New Daylight

Edited by Naomi Starkey   May–August 2008

Suggestions for using *New Daylight*

Find a regular time and place, if possible, where you can read and pray undisturbed. Before you begin, take time to be still and perhaps use the BRF prayer. Then read the Bible passage slowly (try reading it aloud if you find it over-familiar), followed by the comment. You can also use *New Daylight* for group study and discussion, if you prefer.

The prayer or point for reflection can be a starting point for your own meditation and prayer. Many people like to keep a journal to record their thoughts about a Bible passage and items for prayer. In *New Daylight* we also note the Sundays and special festivals from the Church calendar, to keep in step with the Christian year.

New Daylight and the Bible

New Daylight contributors use a range of Bible versions, and you will find a list of the versions used in each issue at the back of the notes on page 154. You are welcome to use your own preferred version alongside the passage printed in the notes, and this can be particularly helpful if the Bible text has been abridged.

New Daylight affirms that the whole of the Bible is God's revelation to us, and we should read, reflect on and learn from every part of both Old and New Testaments. Usually the printed comment presents a straight-forward 'thought for the day', but sometimes it may also raise questions rather than simply providing answers, as we wrestle with some of the more difficult passages of Scripture.

New Daylight is also available in a deluxe edition (larger format). Check out your local Christian bookshop or contact the BRF office, who can also give more details about a cassette version for the visually impaired. For a Braille edition, contact St John's Guild for the Blind, 8 St Raphael's Court, Avenue Road, St Albans, AL1 3EH.

Writers in this issue

Jennifer Oldroyd worked for many years at the Ashburnham Place conference centre in East Sussex. She was Managing Editor for a major Christian publisher and, in the last few years, has had published two books of study material for small groups.

Stephen Rand is a writer and speaker who, in recent years, has shared his time between Jubilee Debt Campaign, persecuted church charity Open Doors, Mainstream (a Baptist church leaders' network) and Kairos Church in Wimbledon. Stephen is the author of BRF's book of Advent readings, *When the Time Was Right*.

David Winter is retired from parish ministry. An honorary Canon of Christ Church, Oxford, he is well known as a writer and broadcaster. He is a Series Editor of *The People's Bible Commentary*.

Rachel Boulding is Deputy Editor of the *Church Times*. Before this, she was Senior Editor at SPCK Publishing and then Senior Liturgy Editor at Church House Publishing. She lives in Dorset with her husband and young son—and, during school terms, more than 70 teenage boys.

Naomi Starkey is the editor of *New Daylight*. She also edits *Quiet Spaces*, BRF's prayer and spirituality journal, as well as commissioning BRF's range of books for adults.

Margaret Silf is an ecumenical Christian, committed to working across and beyond the denominational divides. For most of her working life she was employed in the computer industry, but now devotes herself to writing and accompanying others on their spiritual journey.

John Proctor is married to Elaine, with two adult children. He works for the United Reformed Church, teaching the New Testament to students in Cambridge. John has written *The People's Bible Commentary: Matthew* (BRF, 2001) and booklets on the Gospels in the Grove Biblical Series.

Helen Julian CSF is an Anglican Franciscan sister, a member of the Community of St Francis, and presently serving as Minister Provincial for her community. She has written *Living the Gospel*, *The Lindisfarne Icon* and *The Road to Emmaus* for BRF.

David Robertson has ministered in a variety of parishes since his ordination in 1979 and is currently a vicar in Halifax. He has written *Marriage—Restoring Our Vision* and *Collaborative Ministry* for BRF.

For more in-depth coverage of some of the passages in these
Bible reading notes, we recommend the following titles:

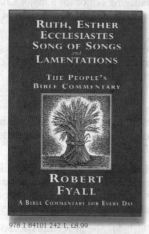

RUTH, ESTHER
ECCLESIASTES
SONG OF SONGS
and
LAMENTATIONS

THE PEOPLE'S
BIBLE COMMENTARY

ROBERT
FYALL

A BIBLE COMMENTARY FOR EVERY DAY

978 1 84101 242 1, £8.99

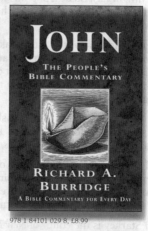

JOHN

THE PEOPLE'S
BIBLE COMMENTARY

RICHARD A.
BURRIDGE

A BIBLE COMMENTARY FOR EVERY DAY

978 1 84101 029 8, £8.99

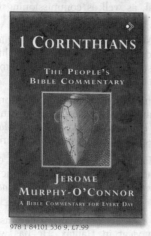

1 CORINTHIANS

THE PEOPLE'S
BIBLE COMMENTARY

JEROME
MURPHY-O'CONNOR

A BIBLE COMMENTARY FOR EVERY DAY

978 1 84101 536 9, £7.99

1 & 2 KINGS

THE PEOPLE'S
BIBLE COMMENTARY

STEPHEN B.
DAWES

A BIBLE COMMENTARY FOR EVERY DAY

978 1 84101 118 9, £7.99

Naomi Starkey writes...

We begin this issue of *New Daylight* with the first of what will be an annual set of readings: Bible passages reflecting themes relevant to the ascension of Jesus to heaven and the coming of the Holy Spirit at Pentecost. For this year, Jennifer Oldroyd has chosen readings from the Gospels and from Acts to explore what she describes as 'the first chapter of the next instalment' of God's dealings with us.

Following on immediately after Jennifer's readings, I am pleased to have Stephen Rand writing two weeks on 'Israel in God's purposes', a topic suggested by a *New Daylight* reader some time ago. As Stephen points out in his introduction, 'Most preachers know that if they want a quiet life, Israel is a topic best avoided', but if we do that, we can end up failing to appreciate our own Jewish heritage as Christians, as well as losing sight of much that is key to understanding the Bible as a whole and the Old Testament in particular.

As well as Stephen's wide-ranging notes, we have a couple of sets of readings taking an in-depth look at key verses or figures in Church history. Margaret Silf considers the 'I am' sayings of Jesus—familiar Gospel verses in which Jesus helps his friends and followers to grasp a little more of who he is and what he came to bring the world. Rachel Boulding spends a week with St Richard of Chichester, choosing

passages from across the Bible that echo themes from his life and from the well-loved prayer ascribed to him.

In putting together this issue, I had a new and somewhat uncomfortable experience. As you may notice from the contents page, I have become a contributor as well as editor—and I realized just how much hard work goes into writing Bible reading notes! After more than six years of dishing out tough assignments to my contributor team, chasing them if they were late with their text and then asking them to redo bits that I judged in need of improvement, I found myself in their shoes (or at their desk) and I was humbled to realize the amount of effort involved.

So I'll finish with three cheers for *New Daylight* contributors, past and present, and a big thank you, once again, to all who write in to encourage us as we continue with our ministry here at BRF.

The BRF Prayer

Almighty God,

you have taught us that your word is a lamp for our feet

and a light for our path. Help us, and all who prayerfully

read your word, to deepen our fellowship with each other

through your love. And in so doing may we come to know you

more fully, love you more truly, and follow more faithfully in

the steps of your son Jesus Christ, who lives and reigns with

you and the Holy Spirit, one God for evermore. Amen.

When the Spirit came

Do you ever daydream about what it would be like if Jesus walked the earth today? Do you ever wonder what he would do—in your neighbourhood, church, home—if he could be physically present?

Sometimes it is so hard to walk in faith and know Jesus only through the scriptures. We are human beings with physical senses and needs. Sometimes we long for him to be here today, to heal and teach and encourage us, rather than just have the promise of his eternal presence in the hereafter.

If that is how we feel today, how much harder it must have been for the disciples as they adjusted to life without Jesus' physical presence. They had known him and loved him. They had followed him and listened to him. After the trauma of his death, they knew the wonder of seeing his face once again, having recognized him in the breaking of bread. They had shared a beach picnic with him and been startled by his sudden appearance as they met together. For six weeks they had got used to this new, amazing, risen Jesus. Then he left.

They stood on the hillside, blinded by the white robes of the angels and their own tears, and faced the prospect that they would not be able to see him, hear him or touch him again. Apart from their memories of the physical Jesus, they then became like us and like all the other disciples from that time to this.

Why did he have to go? Why can he not be present in the world, to build his Church and establish his kingdom? Why does it have to be like this?

For the answers to these questions, we are going to look at what Jesus taught his disciples about the Holy Spirit in John's Gospel. Then we are going to consider the story of the coming of the Holy Spirit in Acts and, finally, still in Acts, we will look at some of the experiences of the apostles in those first few amazing years after Pentecost.

Why were these words and events recorded? So that we and all who follow after can learn what God has ushered in with the death, resurrection and ascension of Jesus. As you begin this next couple of weeks' readings, pray that God the Father will open your eyes to new truths and the amazing things that became possible 'when the Spirit came'.

Jennifer Oldroyd

The Ascension

Now the eleven disciples went to Galilee, to the mountain to which Jesus had directed them. When they saw him, they worshiped him; but some doubted. And Jesus came and said to them, 'All authority in heaven and on earth has been given to me. Go therefore and make disciples of all nations, baptizing them in the name of the Father and of the Son and of the Holy Spirit, and teaching them to obey everything that I have commanded you. And remember, I am with you always, to the end of the age.'

Each of the Gospels describes Jesus' final moments on earth differently. Here, Jesus tells his disciples that all authority in heaven and on earth has been given to him and then he says, 'Go therefore…'. Because he has all authority, because he is King of kings and Lord of lords, those who follow him are to turn outwards to the world and 'make disciples of all nations'.

No matter how we came to faith and no matter what our character and gifts, we all share in that commission. You may be called to leave your country and go in a literal sense. Even if you are housebound or have heavy family responsibilities, though, you cannot escape Jesus' command to 'go'—that is, turn your heart to others and draw them towards the love of God.

Over the next two weeks, we shall discover that the ascension is not the last chapter of the first part of God's amazing story. Rather, it is the first chapter of the next instalment. Now that Jesus has returned to his Father, the Holy Spirit can be poured out on all God's people. The disciples still had no idea what was going to happen and some still had doubts, but, as instructed, they waited and prayed. Maybe as they did so they began to piece together the amazing things Jesus had said about how life would be 'when the Spirit came'. We, too, will go back over Jesus' words in John's Gospel so that, whether we are worshippers or doubters, we can understand God's purposes for the next instalment of his great story.

Prayer

Risen Lord Jesus, we too want to worship you in your ascended glory. We pray for a new understanding of the work of your Spirit in our lives and in our world. Amen

JO

Another Advocate

[Jesus said] 'If you love me, you will keep my commandments. And I will ask the Father, and he will give you another Advocate, to be with you forever. This is the Spirit of truth, whom the world cannot receive, because it neither sees him nor knows him. You know him, because he abides with you, and he will be in you.'

Imagine that a friend of yours has a very important occasion coming up. Perhaps he or she is graduating from university or getting married or ordained or having a child baptized. As a dear friend, you have been invited, but you are unable to go. You phone up or write or visit and explain, 'I am really sorry that I can't come, but I will be thinking of you and will be with you in spirit.'

What does that actually mean to your friend? Probably not a lot! Probably Jesus' disciples felt much the same when he said a similar thing to them. In his case, though, it did mean something. In his case, the person who would be with them 'in spirit' would be 'another Advocate'—a friend and comforter, counsellor and companion. Indeed, he would be all that Jesus had been, and more, and would be with them for ever.

We may think that to have spent time with the physical Jesus must have been amazing and wish that we too could know him 'in person'. In fact, though, the Gospel narrative makes it clear that the disciples did not always understand Jesus, did not always believe him, did not always agree with him. They denied and betrayed him, too. As we saw yesterday, even as they watched the figure of Jesus ascending to the Father, 'some doubted'.

How much better, then, to have this 'other Advocate'. How much better to know for sure, for the rest of our lives—in this world and the next—the presence, comfort, help, advice and friendship of Jesus by means of his Spirit. How much better to have no problem with language, but simply to know, heart to heart, Spirit to spirit, who God is and how much he loves us.

Prayer

Lord Jesus, thank you for asking the Father for this wonderful gift. Help me today to accept the presence and help of your Holy Spirit in my heart and mind. Amen

JO

The Spirit of truth

'This is the Spirit of truth, whom the world cannot receive, because it neither sees him nor knows him. You know him, because he abides with you, and he will be in you.'

Those of us who have belonged to a good local church may well thank God for the training, teaching and mentoring we have received. We may have sat at the feet of a gifted teacher, been encouraged by a wonderful pastor or been part of a small group that has supported and loved us. We may wonder how we would have become the people we are today had it not been for the efforts of these people.

Jesus' disciples felt much the same. They really did not know what would happen if he were to leave them. He has just assured Thomas that he, Jesus, is the way, the truth and the life (v. 6), but then he has also told them that he is going away, so how will they find the way, learn the truth and live the life? For Jesus' disciples, then and now, there is his promise that God will send 'the Spirit of truth' to teach us.

Over the centuries there has been much discussion in the Church about whether 'ordinary people' should be allowed to read the Bible in their native tongue or whether the scriptures should be studied in private by individuals. In Jesus' own day, the rabbinical tradition meant that studying the biblical text was only undertaken with others, so that the truth could be arrived at by consensus and no one would be led astray by their own ideas. There may indeed be a case for submitting our thoughts and ideas to one another, but here is the clear promise of Jesus that the Holy Spirit will be made available to believers and that he is the Spirit of truth.

So, take heart today, especially if your current situation means that you feel you lack adequate biblical teaching. Jesus' promise is that the Spirit of truth will abide with you and be in you and he is able to lead you into all truth as you search the scriptures.

Prayer

Holy Spirit of God, please be my teacher today. Please begin by teaching me how to learn from you and help me to trust you to lead me into all truth. Amen

JO

Not orphaned

'I will not leave you orphaned; I am coming to you. In a little while the world will no longer see me, but you will see me; because I live, you also will live. On that day you will know that I am in my Father, and you in me, and I in you.'

Many will remember the dreadful pictures that came out of Romania after the fall of Ceausescu— orphanages with babies and toddlers tied into cots and left without toys or stimulation of any kind. Their faces were expressionless, their development severely retarded due to lack of human interaction.

In these verses, Jesus promises that even though he will no longer be physically present with his people, we will not be left without love, care and stimulation. Tiny babies need to be fed, changed and given attention. Those born into new life in the kingdom of God need to be fed with the pure milk of God's word. We need the cleansing blood of the Lamb and we need stimulation to grow and develop as we should.

When the Holy Spirit comes to God's people, he comes as a loving parent, offering a relationship that is exemplified in the very best parent—child relationships on earth. 'On that day,' Jesus says, when the Holy Spirit comes to take up his life in us, we will begin to understand the very nature of God and the love that exists between Father, Son and Spirit—a relationship into which we have been drawn and in which we will spend eternity. Because he lives, we will live. Because he loves, we can learn to love.

The departure of the physical Jesus from this world is a plus for us—not a minus. We are not children left without a loving parent and tied by physical restraints into a joyless, loveless, uncaring environment. Rather, we have been adopted out of the orphanage of sin and welcomed into the eternal family relationship that exists within the Godhead.

Reflection and prayer

'As a father has compassion for his children, so the Lord has compassion for those who fear him. For he knows how we were made; he remembers that we are dust' (Psalm 103:13–14).
Pray for a new understanding of the fatherly care and love that God offers his children.

JO

A daily reminder

'I have said these things to you while I am still with you. But the Advocate, the Holy Spirit, whom the Father will send in my name, will teach you everything, and remind you of all that I have said to you.'

A few years before he died, my husband had a stroke, which destroyed his short-term memory. He never knew what day it was or what time of day and we had to find strategies to help him relocate himself in the world. We bought one of those long, narrow calendars, with each day on a new line, and fixed an arrow to a paperclip. The arrow was moved down each day to point at that day's date. All through the day he would constantly refer to that calendar, checking the year, the month and the day, and gaining assurance from knowing where he was in time.

Jesus' words in these two verses remind me of that calendar. When the Spirit comes, he is our point of reference. He comes from the Father, he comes in the name of Jesus, he teaches us and reminds us of Jesus' own words.

When difficult events happen in our lives, we can feel confused, just as the disciples felt confused about Jesus' talk of going away and coming back. Major problems or disasters can leave us reeling, with no point of reference. Great changes can unsettle us. With us and in us, though, we have the Holy Spirit, whose job is to teach us the lessons God has for us and remind us of what he has said and done for us in the past. His work in our lives re-establishes us in the purposes of God. We have no need to let doubt toss us about like a wave on the sea (James 1:6)—we can feel the tug of the anchor of God's love.

Just as my husband would check his calendar at intervals throughout the day, so we can all learn to check for the prompting of the Holy Spirit throughout our day, opening ourselves to his teaching and his gentle direction.

Prayer

O God, draw me back to your presence again and again today. Help me to find my true home in you and my true perspective on the world through your love. Amen

JO

'It's for your own good'

'I did not say these things to you from the beginning, because I was with you. But now I am going to him who sent me; yet none of you asks me, "Where are you going?" But because I have said these things to you, sorrow has filled your hearts. Nevertheless I tell you the truth: it is to your advantage that I go away, for if I do not go away, the Advocate will not come to you; but if I go, I will send him to you. And when he comes, he will prove the world wrong about sin and righteousness and judgement: about sin, because they do not believe in me; about righteousness, because I am going to the Father and you will see me no longer; about judgement, because the ruler of this world has been condemned.'

I suppose it's a hangover from childhood, but if someone tells us that something is for our own good, we are inclined to disagree! In today's passage, Jesus recognizes the sorrow that his disciples are feeling as he talks not only of leaving them but also of the suffering that awaits them (vv. 2–4). Then he tells them that his departure is for their own good and this time we have to agree. Once Jesus, in his physical body, has left the earth with his mission accomplished, the Holy Spirit can move in for the next part of God's plan.

Every day, all over the world, the people of God are persecuted for believing in Jesus. They are ridiculed for being obedient to someone who cannot be seen. This, Jesus says, is only to be expected, but he reminds us that, when the Spirit comes, we will have an Advocate whose job it is to provide us with a defence.

So, if you face problems today—whether physical persecution or simply mild amusement at your faith—spend time tuning in to the Spirit's presence within you, guiding you on how to respond. Jesus himself was only visible to a few people at one brief time in history, in one geographical place. Now that he is risen and ascended, the Advocate is available to every believer, from now until eternity, in every part of the world.

Prayer
Holy Spirit, be with me today. Give me courage, the right words to say and the grace to rely on your counsel. Amen

JO

Behind locked doors

When it was evening on that day, the first day of the week, and the doors of the house where the disciples had met were locked for fear of the Jews, Jesus came and stood among them and said, 'Peace be with you.' After he said this, he showed them his hands and his side. Then the disciples rejoiced when they saw the Lord.

We've looked at some of Jesus' teaching about the Holy Spirit before his death and resurrection. Now we are going to look at some of the things he said in the time between his resurrection and ascension.

The first scene is set on the evening of the day of Jesus' resurrection. The day had begun very early, as you will remember. The disciples had lurched from despair to hope, from hope to amazement and, probably by now, from amazement to a kind of torpor brought on by emotion, exhaustion and fear of the authorities. They were holed up in a house somewhere in Jerusalem with the doors locked. All the same, suddenly Jesus was there.

The story is so familiar to us that we may forget just what effect it would have had on the disciples. Jesus was amazing and they loved him. He had taught them and they had watched his miracles, but, despite all that, he had always been a human being. He ate and slept, walked and talked just like them. Also just like them he had been limited to being in one place at a time. Now, suddenly, he was different. It was the same body, with the marks in his hands and feet that they could hardly bear to look at, but he was no longer subject to human limitations.

Here is our first clue to the new order of the Holy Spirit. He is not subject to human limitations. You knew that, but have you reflected recently on what it means for you, for your family, for your church? Have you experienced what the disciples experienced that late evening? When the Spirit comes, he takes what is 'normal' and familiar and changes it into something amazing. Impossible situations do not hold him and locked doors do not keep him out—he can be with us whenever and wherever we need him.

Prayer

Forgive me, Father, if I have forgotten to expect miracles. Do something unexpected for me today so that my faith in you may grow. Amen

JO

The breath of God

Jesus said to them again, 'Peace be with you. As the Father has sent me, so I send you.' When he had said this, he breathed on them and said to them, 'Receive the Holy Spirit. If you forgive the sins of any, they are forgiven them; if you retain the sins of any, they are retained.'

Some of the most intimate moments between two people who love each other are experienced when they are close enough to feel each other's breath. The disciples would have been taught about the breath of God—in terms of both its life-giving properties (Genesis 2:7) and its power to destroy (Job 4:9). However, they could never have imagined being close enough to God to feel his breath on their cheeks, as close as a nursing child with its mother or as close as a lover.

There, in the lamplight of that locked room in Jerusalem, Jesus leans forward and breathes on them: 'Receive the Holy Spirit.' That breath also blew into Adam's lungs, laid bare the foundations of the world (Psalm 18:15) and blew on the great men and women of the Old Testament, enabling them to do amazing things. Here, it is quietly exhaled on a group of ordinary men.

Jesus continues by explaining that the Holy Spirit will enable them to do extraordinary things.

They are the ones who will implement the next part of God's purposes for the world. Now, through Jesus' death, there is a remedy for sin, but they are the ones who will take that message, to not just their fellow Jews but also the world.

The coming of the Holy Spirit is not to make you feel good or give you a wonderful 'spiritual experience'. Instead, it is to enable you to take into your world the message of the love of God. When did he breathe on them? Immediately after he said to them, 'As the Father has sent me, so I send you…'.

Prayer

Lord Jesus, I did not feel your breath on my face that day, but I praise you today that I can know the breath of God in my life. Inspire (breathe into) me today and, by that living breath, enable me to do what you have called me to do. Amen

JO

The promise of the Father

After his [Jesus'] suffering he presented himself alive to them by many convincing proofs, appearing to them over the course of forty days and speaking about the kingdom of God. While staying with them, he ordered them not to leave Jerusalem, but to wait there for the promise of the Father.

When the Spirit comes, it is as a result of God's plan and purpose from the beginning. There are two references in the Old Testament to God 'pouring out' his Spirit: the prophet Ezekiel speaks of God's promise to pour out his spirit on the house of Israel (39:29) and the prophet Joel speaks of a time when God will pour out his spirit on 'all flesh' (2:28). Peter, in his first sermon on the day of Pentecost, claims that what his audience are witnessing is a fulfilment of the second prophecy—the Spirit available to all.

Before the beginning of time, the Spirit of God 'swept over the face of the waters' (Genesis 1:2). Then came the glorious act that resulted in the created world—the breathing of life into Adam. There was also the fellowship enjoyed between the man, woman and God, but that fellowship was destroyed by sin (3:8).

The rest of the Old Testament is really a description of 'the promise of the Father'. His plans for us have always been about restoring a relationship with him. The death, res-

urrection and ascension of Jesus made that possible and, ever since, the Spirit of God has been able to dwell with and in men and women.

Adam and Eve were able to walk in the garden and enjoy the presence of Almighty God and we, too, can enjoy an amazing fellowship with him. When you sit quietly, praying for the Holy Spirit to come and advise you or encourage you, you are entering into 'the promise of the Father' that Jesus talks about. The creator of the universe, the one whose word brought into being the physical world and who made men and women in order to share that world with him, is the one calling you today to enter in to that relationship with him and inherit the promise that he will indeed 'dwell among us' as our God (see Exodus 29:45–46).

Meditation

Read and meditate on Jeremiah 31:31–34, particularly the phrase, 'I will be their God, and they shall be my people.'

JO

'You will receive power'

So when they [the disciples] had come together, they asked him, 'Lord, is this the time when you will restore the kingdom to Israel?' He replied, 'It is not for you to know the times or periods that the Father has set by his own authority. But you will receive power when the Holy Spirit has come upon you; and you will be my witnesses in Jerusalem, in all Judea and Samaria, and to the ends of the earth.'

Have you ever sat in a church meeting and agreed that what your church or town or area needs is for God to transform people and situations? I certainly have, but study these words of Jesus' carefully.

The disciples knew what was needed to transform their situation: 'Romans out! Israel for ever!' As he so often does, Jesus responds, 'No, but…'. He explains that what is important is not the situation we live in, but the power that is available to us to be his witnesses in that situation.

Is there a drug problem in your neighbourhood? Are youngsters being knifed in the streets of your town? Is teenage pregnancy on the rise? Are you a teacher in a difficult school, a health worker in a deprived area or a minister in the inner city? Do you cry to God daily, 'Are you now going to "restore the kingdom"?' Today, Jesus says to you, 'No, but… you will receive power when the Holy Spirit comes to you and you will be my witnesses.'

Perhaps we need to stop asking God to change things and, instead, ask him to pour out his Holy Spirit on us so that we will receive the power to live as Jesus did. He spoke out against evil and healed people. He demonstrated the righteousness of God and the reality of sin. He brought God's transforming power into every situation. He announced the coming of the kingdom of God. When we receive the power of the Holy Spirit, we may not see our neighbourhood become an outpost of heaven, but we will see men and women transformed as they respond to our witness and meet the living God for themselves.

Prayer

Lord, I cannot be your witness in my own strength. Give me the power I need to testify to your love and show the world a different way.
Amen

JO

Pentecost

When the day of Pentecost had come, they were all together in one place. And suddenly from heaven there came a sound like the rush of a violent wind, and it filled the entire house where they were sitting. Divided tongues, as of fire, appeared among them, and a tongue rested on each of them. All of them were filled with the Holy Spirit and began to speak in other languages, as the Spirit gave them ability.

Wind and fire are two symbols for God's Spirit. The wind can be a gently cooling breeze, lifting the hair from my forehead on a hot day, or drying my washing in the sunshine. It can also be a force so great that roads and bridges are closed, roofs lifted from houses, garden sheds sent spinning down the road.

When it comes to fire, I think of the gentle flames that flicker in my fireplace and warm the room. At other times it can be the roaring storm that engulfs forests, reduces a structure to charcoal and destroys all human and other life in its path.

There are other biblical symbols for God's Spirit—the dove, anointing oil, water. For this occasion, however, when, for the first time, God pours out his Spirit on his people—on everyone in that upper room—he chooses the two symbols wind and fire. This time he is not just bringing blessing or comfort or new life—he is bringing power.

Think about those disciples gathered there in Jerusalem. Fishermen and tax collectors, political agitators and bereaved women, emotionally damaged people desperately trying to make sense of what they had seen and heard over the last three years. They had been given the task of taking to the world the message that they had heard from Jesus. Left to themselves, they might, after a time of recovery and regrouping, have made at least an effort to do what they thought he wanted, but what they needed was the power of the Holy Spirit to enable them. They needed power to preach, power to heal, power to face persecution without giving in —and they got it!

Reflection

'The voice of the Lord flashes forth flames of fire. The voice of the Lord shakes the wilderness' (Psalm 29:7–8). Rejoice that the power of the Lord is available to you through the Holy Spirit. Scared? Good! Excited? Even better!

JO

Right place, right time

Then an angel of the Lord said to Philip, 'Get up and go towards the south to the road that goes down from Jerusalem to Gaza.' (This is a wilderness road.) So he got up and went. Now there was an Ethiopian eunuch, a court official of the Candace, queen of the Ethiopians, in charge of her entire treasury. He had come to Jerusalem to worship and was returning home; seated in his chariot, he was reading the prophet Isaiah. Then the Spirit said to Philip, 'Go over to this chariot and join it.' So Philip ran up to it and heard him reading the prophet Isaiah. He asked, 'Do you understand what you are reading?' He replied, 'How can I, unless someone guides me?' And he invited Philip to get in and sit beside him.

This week we will look at some of the apostles' experiences in the early days as they began to operate in this new dimension of the Spirit and see, in reality, something of what Jesus had promised.

In our passage today, Philip is asked to take a day out from a successful ministry in Samaria (see vv. 5–8) and head off along a 'wilderness road'. He recognizes the voice of God and obeys, whatever his own views are of doing so. Elsewhere in Acts we read of the apostles hearing and obeying the Holy Spirit regarding plans for their evangelistic journeys. When the Spirit comes, he brings something of the life of heaven itself, where the will of God can be clearly known and acted on.

It's Monday and we each face another week of whatever is 'business as usual'. Why don't we make a commitment today to be more sensitive to the Holy Spirit's leading? This week, if we are delayed, diverted or distracted, let's pause and ask ourselves if the Spirit needs us to go on a 'wilderness road' to help another seeking the kingdom of God.

If you have never heard that voice sending you in an unexpected direction, ask God for a fresh experience of his Spirit and make a new commitment to hearing and obeying him.

Prayer

Almighty God, I lay before you my programme for the week. Help me to accomplish what you have planned and, as Philip did, hear and obey your Spirit's call. Amen

JO

The right people for the job

Now during those days, when the disciples were increasing in number, the Hellenists complained against the Hebrews because their widows were being neglected in the daily distribution of food. And the twelve called together the whole community of the disciples and said, 'It is not right that we should neglect the word of God in order to wait at tables. Therefore, friends, select from among yourselves seven men of good standing, full of the Spirit and of wisdom, whom we may appoint to this task, while we, for our part, will devote ourselves to prayer and to serving the word.'

The followers of Jesus are experiencing some amazing times. They have seen large numbers of people pour into the kingdom of God. They have seen members of their group perform miracles of healing. They have faced opposition and persecution. Now they are faced with a more mundane problem: their charitable work among the widows in their community is in disarray.

The apostles could have tackled the problem in various ways. They could have stopped what they were doing, concentrated on getting the aid programme right and earned the gratitude of many. Alternatively, they could have ignored the problem and concentrated on getting the mission strategy right, which might have resulted in even more conversions, but might also have driven a wedge between Hebrew and Greek-speaking Christians.

Instead, they recognized the truth that when the Spirit came,

every person within the kingdom of God became of equal value and every necessary task is assigned by him. Whether it is administering the aid programme or the worship team, the mission planning or the catering for an Alpha supper, the right people for the job are those who are clearly demonstrating the gifts that the Holy Spirit has assigned to them.

There is no longer to be a division, as there was in the temple worship, between the priests and the people. Christ's death has made us all 'to be a kingdom, priests serving his God and Father' (Revelation 1:6).

Prayer
Almighty God, forgive me if I have ignored the gifts with which you have blessed me. Show me what task you have called and equipped me to perform within your Church. Amen

JO

Do I have to?

Now there was a disciple in Damascus named Ananias. The Lord said to him… 'go to the street called Straight, and at the house of Judas look for a man of Tarsus named Saul… he has seen in a vision a man named Ananias come in and lay his hands on him so that he might regain his sight.' But Ananias answered, 'Lord, I have heard from many about this man, how much evil he has done to your saints in Jerusalem; and here he has authority from the chief priests to bind all who invoke your name.' But the Lord said to him, 'Go, for he is an instrument whom I have chosen…' So Ananias went and… laid his hands on Saul and said, 'Brother Saul, the Lord Jesus, who appeared to you on your way here, has sent me so that you may regain your sight and be filled with the Holy Spirit.' And immediately… his sight was restored. Then he got up and was baptized.

It is easy for us to read this story with the benefit of hindsight and rejoice at the conversion of Paul—this key person for the purposes of God—but it was not easy for the Christians of the time. The news of Saul and his campaign to wipe out the followers of Jesus had travelled ahead of him and no doubt Ananias shook in his shoes as he realized what God wanted him to do.

As noted in John, 'the wind blows where it chooses' (3:8), so Ananias and, indeed, the whole Church had to accept that a former enemy had met with Jesus and they were to pray that Paul would be filled with the Holy Spirit. So, not only does Ananias walk into Saul's presence, risking his own life and the lives of all the believers in Damascus, but he also begins by calling him 'brother'.

When the Spirit comes, he gives us brothers and sisters among those we may least expect. We are not to doubt the motives of those whom Christ has called, but open our hearts to them for his sake.

Prayer

Lord Jesus, there are people whom I find it difficult to trust and love. Help me to recognize the work of your Holy Spirit in their lives and learn to call them brother or sister. Amen

JO

Changing the culture

About noon the next day… Peter went up on the roof to pray. He became hungry and wanted something to eat; and while it was being prepared, he fell into a trance. He saw the heaven opened and something like a large sheet coming down, being lowered to the ground by its four corners. In it were all kinds of four-footed creatures and reptiles and birds of the air. Then he heard a voice saying, 'Get up, Peter; kill and eat.' But Peter said, 'By no means, Lord; for I have never eaten anything that is profane or unclean.' The voice said to him again, a second time, 'What God has made clean, you must not call profane.' This happened three times, and the thing was suddenly taken up to heaven.

Many of the stories in Acts seem to suggest that when people experience the Holy Spirit, they don't become different people. Rather, they become more genuinely the people they are. Their character and gifts, skills and personalities are transformed by the touch of the Spirit.

It was Peter—so often the first to speak when Jesus challenged the disciples—who was the first to preach at Pentecost (2:14). Now, it seems, Peter is the first to be challenged by God on how his life must change—and what a change!

For centuries, the Jews had worked on the principle that they were the chosen people and non-Jews were unclean. Those who were not Jews were excluded from worship of God in the temple and it would defile a Jew to visit them or eat with them.

Jesus' death, resurrection and ascension ushered in a new era, however. The way to God has been opened and the veil of the temple torn in two. The Holy Spirit is to be poured out 'on all flesh' (Joel 2:28 and Acts 2:17). Peter said the words, but now he has to learn what they mean. We too can imagine ourselves sitting alongside Peter on that rooftop, and we can ask the Holy Spirit to challenge and inspire us to change in some way. Your reaction may be, like Peter's, 'No, Lord…', but trust him to lead you.

Reflection

Ask God to show you those cultural traditions that the Holy Spirit may want to sweep aside in our time.

JO

In unison

Now in the church at Antioch there were prophets and teachers: Barnabas, Simeon who was called Niger, Lucius of Cyrene, Manaen a member of the court of Herod the ruler, and Saul. While they were worshiping the Lord and fasting, the Holy Spirit said, 'Set apart for me Barnabas and Saul for the work to which I have called them.' Then after fasting and praying they laid their hands on them and sent them off.

The giving of the Holy Spirit at Pentecost happened when 'they were all together in one place' (Acts 2:1). Now, as the work of taking the gospel to the Gentiles was about to get under way, once again God demonstrates that the revelation of his plans will come when his people are united, of one heart and mind and physically meeting together.

There may be differences of character, background or tradition: the group of people named in this passage were Barnabas, a Levite from Cyprus, Simeon, a black man (with the nickname Niger), Lucius, a Roman from Cyrene in North Africa, Manaen, who in his youth was chosen as a companion to a prince, Herod Antipas, and Saul, a Pharisee from Cilicia in southeast Asia Minor. All of these were potential candidates for missionary service.

It was important to all those men—important enough for them to set aside time for prayer and fasting—to worship God and listen to him. In the end, missionaries become such not because they decide they would like to undertake a particular mission, but as the result of the activity of the Holy Spirit by two essential and complementary means: the personal, inward call to the individual and outward confirmation from the Church.

When the Spirit came, he demonstrated through the early Church that, from now on, these two means of communication were to be expected and it is the same for us. We are not simply to rely on our own sense of guidance from God. Nor are we to receive all our direction from the fellowship to which we belong. Rather, we are to regard both as being of equal value and seek both with equal zeal.

Prayer

Father, I commit myself to searching out your will—by means of the voice of the Spirit in my own heart and shared experience with your people.

JO

Made complete

While Apollos was in Corinth, Paul passed through the interior regions and came to Ephesus, where he found some disciples. He said to them, 'Did you receive the Holy Spirit when you became believers?' They replied, 'No, we have not even heard that there is a Holy Spirit.' Then he said, 'Into what then were you baptized?' They answered, 'Into John's baptism.' Paul said, 'John baptized with the baptism of repentance, telling the people to believe in the one who was to come after him, that is, in Jesus.' On hearing this, they were baptized in the name of the Lord Jesus. When Paul had laid his hands on them, the Holy Spirit came upon them, and they spoke in tongues and prophesied—altogether there were about twelve of them.

In the years since John the Baptist's death, his call to repentance had spread to many other places. Here in Ephesus, Paul finds a small fellowship of 12 or so believers who perhaps came to faith as a result of Apollos' teaching (18:24–25). However, their faith is incomplete and they know nothing of new life in Jesus and the gift of the Holy Spirit.

Whatever denomination we belong to, we do well to make quite certain that we have understood and received all that God has prepared for us. The measure of that completeness is the gift of the Holy Spirit, the promise of the Father. When the Spirit comes in power, he brings the development of our spiritual understanding as well as those outward signs of discernment, healing, prophecy and all the other gifts that Paul describes in 1 Corinthians 12. He makes us complete in Christ.

If a modern-day Paul visited your church and asked, 'Did you receive the Holy Spirit when you believed?' what would your answer be? There are many Christians, even today, whose answer would be, 'I think so—I hope so', but we need to be sure. Now more than ever, the Church needs the power and presence of the Holy Spirit. We need him to lead us into all truth, remind us of Jesus' teaching and send us to make disciples of all nations.

Prayer

Heavenly Father, I ask today for a new outpouring of your Holy Spirit. Thank you for promising to answer my prayer. Amen
(See Luke 11:9–13.)

JO

Israel in God's purposes

Most Christians have an opinion about Israel and some are glad to share it! Such opinions have prompted the most vitriolic letters I have ever received. Most preachers know that if they want a quiet life, Israel is a topic best avoided. The sad result is that those with the loudest voices may be the only ones heard and much that is key to our understanding of the Bible is drowned out by them.

So, this fortnight's readings focus on the big picture—God's purpose for his creation. He has been and is still working out that purpose in human history and Israel has a key role in that—and so do you and I!

When human beings rebelled against God, his purpose was—and is—to provide a way to achieve salvation. So, God chose an individual from whom would come a nation. That nation, Israel, was to be the channel for God's revelation to the world and from it came the Son of Man, who was the Son of God. His death on a cross made it possible for his resurrection life to be experienced by all who believe, who are part of the Church of Jesus Christ.

Israel, as God's chosen people, prepared the way for Christ and Christ founded the Church.

Through faith in Christ, Jew and Gentile alike are united in the Church, which is now charged with the responsibility of achieving God's purposes in the world until Christ returns.

So, whatever we think about the place of Jewish people in God's purposes right now, we have to be careful not to underplay the significance of the cross of Jesus. We have to be careful not to assume that the modern state of Israel can, or should be, simply identified with either the Jewish people or the Israel of the Bible.

As Christians, we owe an enormous debt to our Jewish heritage. There is no place or excuse for anti-Semitism. Just as we should make no exceptions for modern-day Israel in our understanding of how a nation state should behave, neither should we make any exceptions for Jewish people in our personal and church relationships. They deserve our love, friendship, respect and the opportunity to meet with Jesus—no more and no less than anyone else. That is certainly part of God's purposes.

Stephen Rand

A seed of hope

And he [God] said, '… Have you eaten from the tree that I commanded you not to eat from?' The man said, 'The woman you put here with me—she gave me some fruit from the tree, and I ate it.' Then the Lord God said to the woman, 'What is this you have done?' The woman said, 'The serpent deceived me, and I ate.' So the Lord God said to the serpent, 'Because you have done this, cursed are you above all livestock and all wild animals! … I will put enmity between you and the woman, and between your offspring and hers; he will crush your head, and you will strike his heel.'

This is the end. Disobeying God's command ended the loving intimacy of the relationship between the Creator God and the human beings made in his image. It ended the unsullied purity of the relationship between human beings. The finger of blame was pointed. It was the end of individuals at ease with themselves as Adam and Eve each refuse to accept responsibility for their actions.

It is also a beginning. It is the beginning of the battle between good and evil that we know all too well from our own experience and which continues to wreak havoc throughout our world. It is the beginning of the battle to survive, having to toil for the food that before had been so readily available in the market garden of Eden. It is the beginning of the battle between the sexes. It is the beginning of the battle with the temptation to selfishly exploit the environment rather than take care of it on behalf of its Creator.

At the moment of horrible failure, though, there is the tiniest seed of hope. It comes as a promise from God that is embedded in his judgment. The one who has prompted the rebellion is told that his victory is ultimately temporary—sin and evil will not have the last word. There will be a descendant of Eve—her 'offspring' (v. 15) —who will 'crush' the source of all that harms, separates and destroys. God will redeem, restore and rebuild—that is his plan and purpose and it will be fulfilled.

Reflection

Thank God that evil does not have the last word—the battle belongs to the Lord.

SR

The blessing of Abraham

The Lord had said to Abram, 'Go from your country, your people and your father's household to the land I will show you. I will make you into a great nation, and I will bless you; I will make your name great, and you will be a blessing. I will bless those who bless you, and whoever curses you I will curse; and all peoples on earth will be blessed through you.' So Abram went, as the Lord had told him; and Lot went with him. Abram was seventy-five years old when he set out from Haran.

Here is step two in God's plan of salvation: the seed of hope is planted. Yesterday we saw how the disobedience of one man brought disaster; today we discover that the obedience of another begins the long journey towards redemption and blessing. Abram—who would be renamed Abraham—stepped out in faith, trusting God and his promises. At the age of 75 he was ready for a new adventure with God!

On the face of it the promise was absurd—the senior citizen with no children was to be the father of a great nation. Yet, Abraham's conviction that God had spoken was sufficient to send him from all the comforts and reassurance of home and family on a journey into the unknown.

The promise revealed a principle. God's great covenant was not simply that Abraham would be the father of a great nation but also that, as they received God's blessing, they would pass that blessing on to others. The tragic history of God's people was that they so readily forgot that they had been chosen to bless *all* peoples.

This principle is specific to God's plan of salvation: 'He redeemed us in order that the blessing given to Abraham might come to the Gentiles through Christ Jesus, so that by faith we might receive the promise of the Spirit' (Galatians 3:14).

It is also a principle for Christian living. What God has done for us is not simply for our own benefit: we receive his blessings—spiritual and material—so that we can share them. We are to be channels—not dams—of his resources of peace. That is God's great purpose.

Prayer

Lord, help us to count our blessings and, even more importantly, help us to share them with others, for Jesus' sake.

SR

Wrestling with God

That night Jacob got up… and crossed the ford of the Jabbok… Jacob was left alone, and a man wrestled with him till daybreak. When the man saw that he could not overpower him, he touched the socket of Jacob's hip so that his hip was wrenched as he wrestled with the man. Then the man said, 'Let me go, for it is daybreak.' But Jacob replied, 'I will not let you go unless you bless me.' The man asked him, 'What is your name?' 'Jacob,' he answered. Then the man said, 'Your name will no longer be Jacob, but Israel, because you have struggled with God and with human beings and have overcome.'

The story moves on. The promise to Abraham is transferred to his son Isaac. Isaac has twins—the younger of which is born grabbing his brother's heel, so is named Jacob as it is a name derived from the Hebrew word for 'heel'. Sure enough, Jacob reveals himself to be a heel as he cheats his brother Esau of his birthright.

On the night of this extraordinary wrestling match, however, Jacob is at the end of his tether. Esau is on his way to meet him with an army of 400 men. Jacob is 'in great fear and distress' (v. 7) and prays to God in desperation 'save me' (v. 11)—reminding God of his promise of a great nation of descendants (v. 12).

It is almost as if his spiritual struggle is given a physical reality here. In the depth of the darkness, Jacob wrestles. Injured, he clings on and demands a blessing. Out of the suffering and apparent defeat, he discovers that God can give a victory—something we learn from the Easter story.

It is a turning point and the change of name denotes a change of character. No longer a cheat and a swindler, now his identity—and that of the nation to be—is defined by the moment he wrestled with God and God blessed him. From this moment on, he relies on God and not his own wiles. It has taken him a long time to get to this point, but, after losing the battle and relying on his own strength, he can now win the victory in God's strength. Learning that really is a blessing.

Reflection

Once we have met with God, we can meet every day and every situation with confidence.

SR

A holy nation

Then Moses went up to God, and the Lord called to him from the mountain and said, 'This is what you are to say to the house of Jacob and what you are to tell the people of Israel: "You yourselves have seen what I did to Egypt, and how I carried you on eagles' wings and brought you to myself. Now if you obey me fully and keep my covenant, then out of all nations you will be my treasured possession. Although the whole earth is mine, you will be for me a kingdom of priests and a holy nation."'

The house of Jacob has become a great nation—the people of Israel. What's more, they have seen God at work in the exodus—his great act of liberating them from slavery in Egypt. Now they are returning to their own land and God speaks to them through Moses, restating and renewing his covenant of promise and purpose.

First, he reminds them that they have seen the evidence of God keeping his side of the agreement. He has acted on their behalf—not just setting them free, but bringing them to himself. However, as in the garden of Eden, there is still the requirement of obedience if the presence and blessing of God are to be retained. This is, after all, a covenant, with two parties entering into an agreement.

The reminder of the covenant promises is accompanied by a reminder of God's purposes for Israel: they are to be a 'holy nation', separated out by God and for God to demonstrate and reveal his purity through their loving service of others; they are to be a 'kingdom of priests', bringing people of all nations to God and God to people of all nations.

Two thousand years later, the apostle Peter wrote and applied these words to the Church—those who had entered in to the new covenant. May God bring them alive for you right now: 'But you are a chosen people, a royal priesthood, a holy nation, God's special possession, that you may declare the praises of him who called you out of darkness into his wonderful light' (1 Peter 2:9).

Prayer

Lord God, as we delight in being your people, help us to live lives of such holiness that others are drawn to your light. Amen

SR

Light in the darkness

This is what God the Lord says—he who created the heavens and stretched them out, who spread out the earth with all that springs from it, who gives breath to its people, and life to those who walk on it: 'I, the Lord, have called you in righteousness; I will take hold of your hand. I will keep you and will make you to be a covenant for the people and a light for the Gentiles, to open eyes that are blind, to free captives from prison and to release from the dungeon those who sit in darkness.'

Isaiah brings God's rebuke to the people of Israel for their failure to see past the religious rituals of worship in the temple and live lives that demonstrate his justice and righteousness. However, Isaiah is also the prophet who clearly and repeatedly looks forward to God fulfilling his covenant purposes by sending his servant, his Messiah, the anointed one who will come from his chosen people.

What a wonderful vision of the fruit of God's intervention in human history is described here! The great Creator, the one who gives life and sustains it, promises his servant the same intimacy of relationship experienced by Adam and Eve when they walked with God in the garden in the cool of the day: 'I will take hold of your hand.' The servant who will suffer will himself be a covenant, bringing people and God together. The resulting transformation will be total. The new life with God will be as different from the old life without him as light is from darkness, as sight is from blindness, as freedom is from imprisonment.

At the moment of judgment and distress for the people of Israel, the prophet looks ahead to the moment when, from their kingly line, will come a servant whose suffering will release a blazing beacon of light that will be for the Gentiles, bringing freedom. Charles Wesley discovered this for himself and his hymn captures the experience so powerfully:

Long my imprisoned spirit lay,
fast bound in sin and nature's night;
Thine eye diffused a quickening ray—
I woke, the dungeon flamed with light;
My chains fell off, my heart was free,
I rose, went forth, and followed Thee.

Prayer

Lord Jesus, let your light shine in my
life. Fill this land with your glory.

SR

Just as he promised

And Mary said: 'My soul glorifies the Lord and my spirit rejoices in God my Saviour, for he has been mindful of the humble state of his servant. From now on all generations will call me blessed, for the Mighty One has done great things for me—holy is his name. His mercy extends to those who fear him, from generation to generation… He has brought down rulers from their thrones but has lifted up the humble. He has filled the hungry with good things but has sent the rich away empty. He has helped his servant Israel, remembering to be merciful to Abraham and his descendants forever, Just as he promised our ancestors.'

Mary has just been told that she is to give birth to the Messiah promised by the prophet Isaiah. The seed of hope we saw planted in Genesis 3:15 on Sunday has born fruit—the 'offspring' has arrived who will 'crush' the source and reality of evil. No wonder, despite all the challenges that this news brings to her, she breaks out into a spontaneous hymn of praise. No wonder this hymn breaks out of the Christmas story into the regular liturgy of the Church.

Mary's magnificent Magnificat praises God because he chooses ordinary people for extraordinary tasks and does great things in and through those humble enough to be open to him. God's blessing is not won by human power and influence, but shared by those who look to him for mercy. This is a God who turns the established order upside down to free the oppressed and establish his Kingdom. He is mighty, he is holy, he is merciful.

God is also to be praised because he is not forgetful. He remembers his promises and keeps them—his purposes are always fulfilled. Mary can trace the thread through the history of Israel and right back to Abraham.

When the baby is born, he is taken to the temple and placed in the arms of Simeon, who is 'waiting for the consolation of Israel' (Luke 2:25). He too praises God for keeping his promises, 'For my eyes have seen your salvation… a light for revelation to the Gentiles and for glory to your people Israel' (vv. 30–32).

Prayer

Loving Father, we echo Mary in praising you because you keep your promises—you have done great things for us. Amen

SR

Not when, but where and who

[Jesus said] 'For John baptized with water, but in a few days you will be baptized with the Holy Spirit.' So when they met together, they asked him, 'Lord, are you at this time going to restore the kingdom to Israel?' He said to them: 'It is not for you to know the times or dates the Father has set by his own authority. But you will receive power when the Holy Spirit comes on you; and you will be my witnesses in Jerusalem, and in all Judea and Samaria, and to the ends of the earth.'

The disciples had been with Jesus for three years. They had followed him as he made his triumphal entry into Jerusalem. They had seen the injustice of his show trial, his suffering and his awful death. Now they were witnesses to the glory of his resurrection.

However, their horizons were still parochial, their understanding confined by their culture and longing to see the hated invader driven from the land. With Jesus back, their hopes have been renewed and they ask, is now the moment for the restoration of Israel?

Rather than rebuke them for asking this question, Jesus answers in a way that is entirely consistent with all that God revealed to Israel in the course of 2000 years. Abraham had been told that all peoples on earth would be blessed through him; now this group of his descendants are told that they will be empowered by God's Spirit to fulfil that part of God's promise, his original plan and purpose.

So, Jerusalem, the great city at the heart of the Jewish nation, was still part of the plan, but it was a starting point, not the objective. They were to go to Samaria, to the very people they had learned to reject and avoid for their history and theology. In fact, everyone, everywhere was to be included. They were to be witnesses of, and for, Jesus—the one who spoke to Samaritan women in public, healed the children of occupying troops and spoke to Gentiles in between spending time with quislings and prostitutes. That was how the kingdom would be restored to Israel.

Reflection

Praise God for the geographical and social inclusiveness of his kingdom as it means there is room for me and you!

SR

A light for the Gentiles

On the next sabbath almost the whole city gathered to hear the word of the Lord. When the Jews saw the crowds, they were filled with jealousy. They began to contradict what Paul was saying and heaped abuse on him. Then Paul and Barnabas answered them boldly: 'We had to speak the word of God to you first. Since you reject it and do not consider yourselves worthy of eternal life, we now turn to the Gentiles. For this is what the Lord has commanded us: "I have made you a light for the Gentiles, that you may bring salvation to the ends of the earth."'

The book of Acts reveals exactly how the last words of Jesus were worked out by the disciples. On the day of Pentecost, they receive power through God's Holy Spirit, witness that Jesus is God's chosen Messiah to the great crowd in Jerusalem and the Church is born. Because Jerusalem is packed with visitors from across the known world, from day one the Church is multilingual and multi-ethnic.

From that point, it is persecution that drives them out from their own religion and culture. In Acts 8:1, the apostles remain in Jerusalem, but believers are forced into Judea and Samaria. Then their persecutor Saul becomes the great missionary apostle Paul, travelling throughout Asia Minor (modern Turkey) and on to Greece and Rome.

His strategy is consistent. He heads for the synagogue, makes as much progress among the Jewish people as he can and, when that fails, moves on to the Gentiles. However, that very willingness to engage with the Gentiles infuriates the Jews and causes deep tensions within the Church.

In today's reading the leaders of the synagogue in Pisidian Antioch had invited Paul and Barnabas to speak, but the mass turnout the following week was too much for them. So, Paul is prompted to articulate clearly that he is following the Lord's command because he is following the Lord. It was the suffering servant in Isaiah who was to be a light to the Gentiles (Isaiah 49:6) and Simeon applied those words to the infant Jesus (Luke 2:32). Now, Paul, as a follower of Jesus, takes that mantle on himself.

Prayer

Loving Father, help us to be followers of Jesus in word and deed, so that we may be lights for the world. Amen

SR

One new humanity

Therefore, remember that formerly you who are Gentiles by birth… were separate from Christ, excluded from citizenship in Israel and foreigners to the covenants of the promise, without hope and without God in the world. But now in Christ Jesus you who once were far away have been brought near through the blood of Christ… His purpose was to create in himself one new humanity out of the two, thus making peace, and in one body to reconcile both of them to God through the cross… Consequently, you are no longer foreigners and strangers, but fellow citizens with God's people and also members of his household.

There were few, if any, greater barriers in the ancient world than those between Jew and Gentile. The whole Jewish culture was designed to maintain the distinction. They were God's chosen people and that had to be made clear in the way they ate, dressed, went about their business and worshipped.

Just as there was an enormous gulf to be crossed by Jewish believers if they were to come to terms with Gentiles entering into the promise of salvation they had thought was reserved solely for them, there was an equally large gulf to be bridged by Gentile believers. Any that had been in contact with those who worshipped the God of the Jews were used to being thought inadequate, outsiders, inferior. They were not familiar with the religious behaviour that Jews followed as second nature.

So, Paul writes to these Gentile Christians in Ephesus, explaining in the strongest possible terms that, although they had been on the outside, they are now on the inside. What's more, they do not have to become Jewish to be accepted. God made possible 'one new humanity' into which Jewish and Gentile believers enter on equal terms—due to the blood Jesus shed on the cross.

God made peace. There was now a new relationship with God and a new reconciled relationship between Jew and Gentile. They are now fellow citizens, members of God's household. Only God could have done this. It was why Jesus came and why Jesus died.

Reflection

What are the barriers between people in today's society? Could I and could the Church do more to help people feel no longer strangers?

SR

Children of the promise

I have great sorrow and unceasing anguish in my heart... for the sake of my people, those of my own race, the people of Israel. Theirs is the adoption; theirs the divine glory, the covenants, the receiving of the law, the temple worship and the promises. Theirs are the patriarchs, and from them is traced the human ancestry of the Messiah, who is God over all, forever praised! Amen. It is not as though God's word had failed. For not all who are descended from Israel are Israel. Nor because they are his descendants are they all Abraham's children. On the contrary... it is not the natural children who are God's children, but it is the children of the promise who are regarded as Abraham's offspring.

Paul was the apostle to the Gentiles, but he felt the rejection of his message by his own people deeply. It not only caused him personal pain but it was also frustratingly baffling. They had received every incentive to believe. They had been chosen, had seen the glory of God at work as he made his covenant and kept his promises. What was more, the family line of the Messiah included the great men of God in the nation's history. That was why Jesus could say 'salvation is from the Jews' (John 4:22).

However, Paul was equally insistent that being born Jewish was not enough in itself to guarantee God's acceptance. Just as Jesus had insisted to Nicodemus that 'no one can see the kingdom of God unless he is born again' (John 3:3), so Paul emphasizes that 'it is not the natural children who are God's children.' His argument is partly simple logic. Abraham had more than one child, but God's promises were only passed down through one, Isaac. In that sense, therefore, only Isaac's descendants were children of the promise.

There is also a deeper spiritual truth here. Paul indicates that there is a different way of defining 'Israel'. In Galatians 6:15–16 he writes, 'Neither circumcision nor uncircumcision means anything; what counts is a new creation... the Israel of God.' All who believe, whether Jew or Gentile, are born again into God's kingdom. They become the children of the promise and are truly Israel. Now that is good news.

Prayer

Thank you, Father, that you call us your children.

SR

ROMANS 10:1, 9–13 (TNIV)

No difference

Brothers and sisters, my heart's desire and prayer to God for the Israelites is that they may be saved... That if you confess with your mouth, 'Jesus is Lord,' and believe in your heart that God raised him from the dead, you will be saved. For it is with your heart that you believe and are justified, and it is with your mouth that you profess your faith and are saved. As Scripture says, 'Anyone who believes in him will never be put to shame.' For there is no difference between Jew and Gentile—the same Lord is Lord of all and richly blesses all who call on him, for, 'Everyone who calls on the name of the Lord will be saved.'

Paul's letter to the Romans is all about how people can be put right with God. Sin has broken the relationship with God and brought death, which is 'the wages of sin' (6:23). This applies to everyone: 'There is no difference, for all have sinned and fall short' (3:22–23).

He has also insisted that faith in Christ is the key to life: 'we have been justified through faith, we have peace with God through our Lord Jesus Christ, through whom we have gained access by faith into this grace in which we now stand' (5:1–2). So, when he repeats his deepest longing that his own people should be saved from the consequences of sin, he is completely consistent: 'there is no difference between Jew and Gentile' (10:12). The problem and the solution are the same for both.

Becoming a Christian meant saying for everyone to hear, 'Jesus is Lord'. It was important that they also believed those words, but there was every reason for them to. Jewish believers were explicitly rejecting their cultural and theological heritage, using the word reserved exclusively for God that was never to be spoken—they were saying 'Jesus is God.' Equally, a Roman convert would be all too aware that the Emperor could demand that he was called Lord and might not take kindly to being usurped by a crucified Jewish criminal.

There was no difference for believers. To Jew and Gentile, salvation came from having the faith to risk all, break with the past and trust God for the future.

Reflection

Jesus is Lord; Jesus is alive. Is this any easier to say and believe now than it was then?

SR

The chosen few

I ask then: Did God reject his people? By no means! I am an Israelite myself, a descendant of Abraham, from the tribe of Benjamin. God did not reject his people, whom he foreknew. Don't you know what Scripture says in the passage about Elijah—how he appealed to God against Israel: 'Lord, they have killed your prophets and torn down your altars; I am the only one left, and they are trying to kill me'? And what was God's answer to him? 'I have reserved for myself seven thousand who have not bowed the knee to Baal.' So too, at the present time there is a remnant chosen by grace. And if by grace, then it cannot be based on works; if it were, grace would no longer be grace.

The fact that salvation has come to the Gentiles does not mean that God has rejected the Jews. Even though as a nation they had rejected God, he did not given up on them. 'There's a simple proof of that,' says Paul, 'just look at me! I was a Jew enthusiastically persecuting every Christian I could find, yet God met me and included me in his purposes and his salvation. If God was rejecting his people, he would certainly have rejected me.'

Then Paul appeals to Jewish history for a further example. At a moment of great crisis, when Elijah thought that he was the only one left who remained faithful, he was told that there was a significant number still with him. They were unknown to Elijah, but known to God.

This is a truth that is highly relevant to the contemporary world. Each month I write about persecuted parts of the Church around the world and each day emails arrive with stories of suffering and loss. While writing these notes, I heard of four Christians who had been murdered in a country with virtually no Christians at all. However, God has promised that his Church will come from every tribe and nation, so it is worth repeating that, however dark the situation, sin and evil do not have the last word.

Paul believed that God's mercy and grace are always available, whether to the great multitude of believers or to the chosen few.

Prayer

Lord, in situations where all seems lost, encourage your people and strengthen them with the knowledge that you have not given up on them.

SR

All Israel

Consider therefore the kindness and sternness of God: sternness to those who fell, but kindness to you, provided that you continue in his kindness. Otherwise, you also will be cut off. And if they do not persist in unbelief, they will be grafted in, for God is able to graft them in again. After all, if you were cut out of an olive tree that is wild by nature, and contrary to nature were grafted into a cultivated olive tree, how much more readily will these, the natural branches, be grafted into their own olive tree!… Israel has experienced a hardening in part until the full number of the Gentiles has come in, and in this way all Israel will be saved.

God had not turned his back on the Jewish people, nor would he. The offer of salvation remained open to them, 'for God is able to graft them in again' (v. 23).

Paul is clear all that has happened is part of God's plan, all is subject to God's sovereignty. Salvation is not a random divine whim that we might latch on to by luck or by being in the right place at the right time. No, 'God is working his purpose out' as one hymn puts it.

To human minds it may be puzzling—Paul calls it a 'mystery'. God chose Israel, hardened their hearts, then included the Gentiles so that Israel would be jealous and prompted to turn to Christ and receive what God had wanted and intended them to receive all along.

What did Paul mean, though, when he said 'all Israel will be saved'? It's a problem! Some have said that he must mean the 'spiritual' Israel—all who have come to God through Christ. Others believe he must mean every single Jew. However, neither of these is entirely consistent with Paul's argument here and in his other writings.

I think that the answer may lie in both the concept of Israel as a nation being more than the total sum of its individual members and Paul's unswerving belief in the mercy and grace of God in working out his purposes. That is a solid foundation when faced with a mystery.

Reflection

Do we share Paul's longing to see Jews and Gentiles alike all coming to God, united by faith in the family of Christ?

SR

To God be the glory!

Oh, the depth of the riches of the wisdom and knowledge of God! How unsearchable his judgments, and his paths beyond tracing out! 'Who has known the mind of the Lord? Or who has been his counsellor? Who has ever given to God, that God should repay them?' For from him and through him and to him are all things. To him be the glory forever! Amen.

The apostle Paul has been wrestling with a complicated theological and philosophical problem. He is not just intellectually exhausted as a result—this is a deeply spiritual and emotional experience. It is the eternal destiny of his own people that is at stake.

The language he has used in chapters 9—11 indicates just how much this matters to him. Indeed, he began this section by saying, 'I have great sorrow and unceasing anguish in my heart' (9:2). So, perhaps amazingly, he finishes it with a glorious hymn of praise to a glorious God. He has been trying to unravel and explain a 'mystery' (11:25) and, in preparing these readings, I can certainly identify with that! Faced with this daunting challenge, which has stretched his mind and spirit to the limit, Paul is moved to worship. As James R. Edwards puts it, 'Where the legs of reason grow weary, the heart may yet soar on wings like eagles' (*New International Bible Commentary: Romans*, Paternoster Press, 1995).

At the end of chapter 8, as he prepared to write about God's dealings with Israel, past and future, Paul wrote powerfully and movingly that there was nothing which could separate God's people from his all-encompassing love. Now he reaffirms his faith in God, absolutely confident that nothing is too great for his wisdom and knowledge, even though there may be things beyond human understanding.

Whatever your views may be on the role and place of Israel in God's purposes, my prayer is that you will be sure of your place in God's purposes, surrounded and supported by his love, confident of his wisdom, ready and willing to worship him. As Fanny Crosby's great old hymn says, 'To God be the glory, great things he has done.'

Prayer

Lord God, help me to know and understand and always to worship you. Thank you for including me in your great plan of salvation. Amen

SR

The book of Ruth

We are about to read one of the Bible's great stories—a story of human loyalty and kinship, a heart-warming reminder that human beings are capable of rising above tribal, ethnic and language barriers to embrace each other as children of the one God. It is also a story that speaks with peculiar relevance in a contemporary world where migration is common, yet a divisive issue—a world of 'illegal immigrants' and 'economic migration', where 'alien' is still often used as a term of abuse.

The story is about one family of Jews, who migrated from Bethlehem in Judah to Moab (the land we now call Jordan) during a time of famine in Israel. There, tragedy befell them. The head of the family, Elimelech, died, leaving his wife, Naomi, a widow. Her two sons married Moabite women—Orpah and Ruth—but then they too died. That left Naomi on her own with her two daughters-in-law, neither of them Jewish.

The story unfolds from that point into a touching narrative of human emotions and responses, all set within a culture that was clearly archaic by the time the book was written—'in the days when the judges ruled', according to the opening of the book. There is scholarly argument about when this story is set in the history of Israel, but the most likely period for its composition seems to be between the 8th and 10th centuries BC. This would mean that it relates events occurring a considerable time before that—before there was a king in Israel. Without giving the game away, the end of the book would be meaningless if it were not describing events before David's glorious reign.

This is not a book full of devotional insights or theological propositions. Rather, it's a book about people relating to each other under God. Well, perhaps that is, in a way, both profoundly theological and devotional!

At its heart, though, this is a story that is told with masterly skill. It unfolds bit by bit, with twists and turns. For anyone reading it for the first time, there are surprises and even shocks in store! What is certain is that it has three heroic figures in it, but I think I should leave you to decide who they are.

David Winter

Ruth 1:1–5 (NRSV)

The story begins

In the days when the judges ruled, there was a famine in the land, and a certain man of Bethlehem in Judah went to live in the country of Moab, he and his wife and two sons. The name of the man was Elimelech and the name of his wife Naomi, and the names of his two sons were Mahlon and Chilion; they were Ephrathites from Bethlehem in Judah. They went into the country of Moab and remained there. But Elimelech, the husband of Naomi, died, and she was left with her two sons. These took Moabite wives; the name of the one was Orpah and the name of the other Ruth. When they had lived there about ten years, both Mahlon and Chilion also died, so that the woman was left without her two sons and her husband.

It's always a challenge to go and live in a 'foreign' land. We may struggle with the language or customs, find the people hard to relate to, the diet may not suit us—and all that may apply to the longed-for 'place in the sun' just across the Channel!

For Naomi, life must have seemed quite desperate after her husband and then her sons died, leaving her a conspicuous alien in a foreign land, honouring a different god, speaking a different language, following a different way of life. She had two daughters-in-law and doubtless she loved them, if only for her sons' sakes, but they were Moabites. They did not know or follow the God of Abraham, Isaac and Jacob. They were not Jews by birth and their religion and culture were not hers. Naomi must, at that moment, have felt very alone.

The cultures and religions of Moab and Judah were poles apart. Psalms describes Moab as God's 'washpot' (60:8, KJV)—hardly the language of good neighbours! It was a famine that had brought Naomi and her family to Moab, but being starved of the familiar would surely draw her back home.

Reflection
There are times for most of us when we feel like strangers, even in our own land. Perhaps we have moved house, started a new job or found ourselves in an environment where our faith is ridiculed or rejected. How can we find security and peace of mind in such a situation?
Read on!

DW

Decision time

Then she [Naomi] started to return with her daughters-in-law from the country of Moab, for she had heard… that the Lord had had consideration for his people and given them food. So she set out from the place where she had been living, she and her two daughters-in-law, and they went on their way to go back to the land of Judah. But Naomi said to her two daughters-in-law, 'Go back each of you to your mother's house. May the Lord deal kindly with you, as you have dealt with the dead and with me…' Then she kissed them, and they wept aloud. They said to her, 'No, we will return with you to your people.' But Naomi said, 'Turn back, my daughters, why will you go with me? Do I still have sons in my womb that they may become your husbands? Turn back, my daughters, go your way, for I am too old to have a husband.'

When Naomi heard that the famine in Judah was over, the familiar landscape and people of home proved irresistible and she decided to go back to Bethlehem. Her daughters-in-law were still young women, of course, and she assumed that they would wish to stay in their own land and marry again. Probably to her surprise, they said that they would come with her. There were tears and hugs all round, but Naomi was a wise woman and she could see that what they were proposing was simply not in their best interests. If they came back with her, they would forfeit the opportunity of marriage. Marriage to a Gentile would be frowned on and she was too old to have any more sons for them to marry. 'Stay', she advised them.

Naomi prayed that the Lord would 'deal kindly' with them as they had dealt kindly with her two dear sons. They had been good wives and were also obviously loving and caring daughters-in-law. Her advice, in other words, was not based on self-interest, but on the welfare of these two young Moabite women.

Reflection

Naomi was a strong-minded woman—a true survivor. That inner strength enabled her to set aside her own self-interest and focus on Ruth and Orpah's situation. Sometimes the hardest thing in the world is doing what we know to be right when our own advantage lies elsewhere.

DW

Ruth's pledge

And they lifted up their voice and wept again: and Orpah kissed her mother-in-law; but Ruth clave unto her. And she [Naomi] said, 'Behold, thy sister-in-law is gone back unto her people, and unto her gods: return thou after thy sister-in-law'. And Ruth said, 'Intreat me not to leave thee, or to return from following after thee: for whither thou goest, I will go; and where thou lodgest, I will lodge: thy people shall be my people, and thy God my God: Where thou diest, will I die, and there will I be buried: the Lord do so to me, and more also, if ought but death part thee and me'. When she saw that she was stedfastly minded to go with her, then she left speaking unto her.

I found it impossible to present this particular passage of Ruth in anything but the ringing words of the King James Version. Ruth's pledge to Naomi is classical in style, with its dramatic climax expressed in a series of poetic and rhythmic phrases. Only this translation seems adequately to capture its elegance. Perhaps the writer wanted to convey a sophistication and eloquence about this young Moabite woman that would justify her exalted role in the subsequent future of Israel.

In fact, Ruth was sacrificing all the most precious elements of the culture she lived in—home, family, religion. She would even forfeit her fundamental right to be buried among her own people. This sacrifice, apparently freely and gladly given, was for the sake of an elderly, destitute and foreign widow, who was in no position to offer her anything in return. No wonder her actions are seen as a supreme example of love and loyalty.

Ruth's decision would have surprised and moved its first hearers, especially as the Moabites were ancient enemies of the Jews. I heard a sermon years ago by a young ordinand who preached on this passage in the presence of her Hindu parents. She spoke of love and loyalty, family ties and the bonds of faith, what it meant to 'leave' and to 'cleave'. Her parents, both medical doctors, told me afterwards how proud they were of her because, like Ruth, she was following both head and heart in accordance with her conscience.

Reflection
Ruth's pledge is a challenge to half-hearted commitment and 'qualified' loyalty.

DW

The bitterness of loss

So the two of them went on until they came to Bethlehem. When they came to Bethlehem, the whole town was stirred because of them; and the women said, 'Is this Naomi?' She said to them, 'Call me no longer Naomi, call me Mara, for the Almighty has dealt bitterly with me. I went away full, but the Lord has brought me back empty; why call me Naomi when the Lord has dealt harshly with me, and the Almighty has brought calamity upon me?' So Naomi returned together with Ruth the Moabite, her daughter-in-law, who came back with her from the country of Moab. They came to Bethlehem at the beginning of the barley harvest.

Bethlehem was not a large place in those days and many people would have known Naomi from the time before she left for Moab with her husband and sons. Now—with the famine over—she was back, but accompanied only by a young Moabite woman, whom she presumably introduced as her daughter-in-law. When the neighbours heard her story they were 'stirred' by it. Certainly the sequence of calamities that had befallen her would have evoked sympathy, although it is possible that some may have baulked at the thought of her sons taking Moabite women for wives and bringing one of them back with her to Judah.

Naomi herself saw all that had happened in her life as a judgment from God. He had 'dealt harshly' with her, she says. She had gone away 'full', and had returned 'empty'. Her given name was Naomi, which means 'sweet', but she felt that his judgment meant that she should take a more appropriate name—Mara, which means 'bitter'. Naomi's belief that all that had happened was a judgment from God was completely in line with the Hebrew view of cause and effect—everything everywhere was brought about by the direct acts of God, which would have included her triple bereavement. She was not saying that she felt bitter, but that the Almighty had dealt 'bitterly' with her.

Reflection

When we read the New Testament, we find that it offers a rather different view of providence. God is seen to work within the events of our lives for our good rather than being the direct instigator of them (see Romans 8:28).

DW

'As it happened…'

Now Naomi had a kinsman on her husband's side, a prominent rich man, of the family of Elimelech, whose name was Boaz. And Ruth the Moabite said to Naomi, 'Let me go to the field and glean among the ears of grain, behind someone in whose sight I may find favour.' She said to her, 'Go, my daughter.' So she went. She came and gleaned in the field behind the reapers. As it happened, she came to the part of the field belonging to Boaz, who was of the family of Elimelech. Just then Boaz came from Bethlehem. He said to the reapers, 'The Lord be with you.' They answered, 'The Lord bless you.'

From this point, the story shifts its emphasis. Naomi and Ruth have come to Bethlehem—a destitute widow and her foreign daughter-in-law. Their only hope of security lies in Naomi's family ties. Jewish law laid considerable responsibilities on the male relatives of a widow, so it was not unreasonable for Naomi to look around and consider the possibilities. On her husband's side, there was a rich relative ('rich' being an important qualification for a benefactor) called Boaz. The question now became one of how he could be alerted to their plight without making a direct appeal for help?

Naomi was resourceful and the rest of the story concerns her plan—one hesitates to call it a plot—to establish a relationship with Boaz. She evidently decides that Ruth, who may well have been an attractive young woman, would be the best point of contact. During the barley harvest (just after Passover), there was a period when poorer people could glean the corners of the fields and Ruth was keen to do this. Naomi's approval seems confirmation that this was no casual decision—it could be Boaz's field and Ruth would glean behind someone in whose sight she 'may find favour'.

So, 'as it happened' seems a slightly disingenuous way of describing what took place. Ruth went to the right field, gleaned with the right young women and eventually caught the eye of Boaz.

Reflection

Boaz's greeting to the gleaners is beautiful in its simplicity: 'The Lord be with you'. Their answer rang across the field: 'The Lord bless you!' Here is a rural community going about its daily life, knowing the reality and presence of God.

DW

The reward of diligence

Then Boaz said to his servant who was in charge of the reapers, 'To whom does this young woman belong?' The servant who was in charge of the reapers answered, 'She is the Moabite who came back with Naomi from the country of Moab. She said, "Please, let me glean and gather among the sheaves behind the reapers." So she came, and she has been on her feet from early this morning until now, without resting even for a moment.' Then Boaz said to Ruth, 'Now listen, my daughter, do not go to glean in another field or leave this one, but keep close to my young women. Keep your eyes on the field that is being reaped, and follow behind them. I have ordered the young men not to bother you. If you get thirsty, go to the vessels and drink from what the young men have drawn.'

The plot thickens! As Naomi had doubtless hoped, Boaz noticed her gleaning very diligently behind his reapers and asked his servant about her. After being told who she was and her relationship to Naomi, his kinswoman, he approached her himself. His invitation to her is an encouraging one. She could assume a privileged position compared with the other gleaners, working alongside his own young women. Indeed, he advised her not to go to any other field—why would she, when all her hopes and Naomi's were pinned on the expectation that this man would meet his responsibilities to them as his kinsfolk?

Boaz went a little further. Ruth could consider herself 'part of the team', as it were, sharing in the refreshments provided for them and protected by the direct orders of Boaz from any harassment from the young men, who perhaps regarded the casual gleaners as fair game. Boaz even addressed her in affectionate terms as 'my daughter'. Surely all of this could only be a sign that things for the widow and her foreign daughter-in-law were destined to improve?

Reflection

'And whoever does not provide for relatives, and especially for family members, has denied the faith and is worse than an unbeliever' (1 Timothy 5:8). Clearly, a godly concern for our own kinsfolk is not simply an archaic notion from the days of the judges. Naomi would certainly agree with this Christian apostle!

DW

The welcome immigrant

Then she [Ruth] fell prostrate, with her face to the ground, and said to him, 'Why have I found favour in your sight, that you should take notice of me, when I am a foreigner?' But Boaz answered her, 'All that you have done for your mother-in-law… has been fully told me, and how you left your father and mother and your native land and came to a people that you did not know before. May the Lord reward you for your deeds, and may you have a full reward from the Lord, the God of Israel, under whose wings you have come for refuge!' Then she said, 'May I continue to find favour in your sight, my lord, for you have comforted me and spoken kindly to your servant, even though I am not one of your servants.'

If Ruth's pledge is one of the key verses in this book, Boaz's prayer for Ruth is the other. In response to his kind words in yesterday's reading, she fell prostrate to the ground before him—a sign of submission—and expressed her gratitude in words of touching humility. Why should the rich landowner act so kindly to her, a foreigner?

His answer is revealing. He had been fully informed of her loyalty to Naomi and her courage in coming to a foreign land, adapting to its customs and accepting its religion. He then prayed for her: 'May the Lord reward you for your deeds, and may you have a full reward from the Lord, the God of Israel, under whose wings you have come for refuge!' The immigrant is prayed for as a member of the covenant community—the people who live under the wings of Yahweh, the Lord.

Ruth's response picks up the theme of 'favour' that she had mentioned earlier. The word is akin to the New Testament notion of 'grace'—undeserved favour. Boaz had dealt kindly with her and brought her comfort, so that she could speak of herself as his 'servant', even though she was not one of the young women of his household.

Reflection

Naomi felt that God had dealt harshly with her. In contrast, Ruth recognizes that Boaz has dealt kindly with her. These are the first signs that, despite the sad circumstances that had brought the two women to Bethlehem, there may yet be a happy ending.

DW

RUTH 2:19–23 (NRSV, ABRIDGED)

Not forsaken, but blessed

Her mother-in-law [Naomi] said to her, 'Where did you glean today? And where have you worked? Blessed be the man who took notice of you.' So she told her mother-in-law with whom she had worked, and said, 'The name of the man... is Boaz.' Then Naomi said to her daughter-in-law, 'Blessed be he by the Lord, whose kindness has not forsaken the living or the dead!' Naomi also said to her, 'The man is a relative of ours, one of our nearest kin.' Then Ruth the Moabite said, 'He even said to me, "Stay close by my servants, until they have finished all my harvest."' Naomi said to Ruth, her daughter-in-law, 'It is better, my daughter, that you go out with his young women, otherwise you might be bothered in another field.' So she stayed close to the young women of Boaz, gleaning until the end of the barley and wheat harvests; and she lived with her mother-in-law.

Naomi knew that she had a rich kinsman in Bethlehem, a landowner called Boaz, and, in agreeing to Ruth gleaning in the fields, she must have hoped that some kind of contact would have been made with him. So, when Ruth returned at night with food given to her by Boaz himself, Naomi's delight would have known no bounds: 'Blessed be he by the Lord, whose kindness has not forsaken the living or the dead!' Boaz had recognized, she felt sure, his obligation to his kinsmen Elimelech, Mahlon and Chilion, who had died, and to Naomi and Ruth, who were living. She reminded Ruth of his kinship, but did not use the legal term for that of go'el, 'kinsman redeemer', whose responsibility was to provide for his relative's widow.

Ruth explained how attentive and kind Boaz had already been. Indeed, he had singled her out for special attention. Naomi doubtless noted all this, but simply advised her daughter-in-law to 'keep close' to Boaz's young women and stay in his fields where she would be safe. This she obediently did, right through to the end of the harvest.

Reflection

In today's language, one suspects that Boaz 'fancied' Ruth, but he, Ruth and Naomi would also have been aware of the deep significance of the extended family as a social and moral framework. Love and duty can combine!

DW

Seeking security

Naomi her mother-in-law said to her, 'My daughter, I need to seek some security for you, so that it may be well with you. Now here is our kinsman Boaz, with whose young women you have been working. See, he is winnowing barley tonight at the threshing floor. Now wash and anoint yourself, and put on your best clothes and go down to the threshing floor; but do not make yourself known to the man until he has finished eating and drinking. When he lies down, observe the place where he lies; then, go and uncover his feet and lie down; and he will tell you what to do.' She [Ruth] said to her, 'All that you tell me I will do.'

Naomi was concerned for Ruth's future security. After all, she had left her home and people to accompany her mother-in-law to Bethlehem and would presumably one day be left alone, an unmarried woman in an alien land. It was time to begin thinking about 'security' for her, which simply means a home and a husband. Boaz is the obvious prime candidate—a wealthy landowner and near kinsman who has already shown the young woman 'kindness'. Naomi could have pointed out the benefits, but Ruth was probably already aware of them.

The older woman set out her plan. That night the barley was being winnowed on the local threshing floor. When the task was completed there were celebrations and the participants, including Boaz, would be in a good mood. Ruth was to wash and anoint herself with perfumed oil, put on her best clothes and make her way to the threshing floor. She should observe where Boaz chose to lie down to sleep (it was customary for the owner to sleep alongside the threshed grain to discourage pilfering).

Once Boaz had fallen asleep, Ruth was to 'uncover his feet'—a euphemism, needless to say, for something a little more daring—and lie down beside him. Naomi was confident that he would then tell her what to do next.

Reflection

All of this sounds like a plot to ensnare poor Boaz, but, as a near kinsman, he would not have seen it that way. All the participants in this little drama would have seen its events and its eventual outcome as being 'under God', the Lord, 'under whose wings' Naomi and Ruth had come for refuge.

DW

Loyal and worthy

When Boaz had eaten and drunk, and he was in a contented mood, he went to lie down at the end of the heap of grain. Then she [Ruth] came quietly and uncovered his feet, and lay down. At midnight the man was startled, and turned over, and there, lying at his feet, was a woman! He said, 'Who are you?' And she answered, 'I am Ruth, your servant; spread your cloak over your servant, for you are next-of-kin.' He said, 'May you be blessed by the Lord, my daughter; this last instance of your loyalty is better than the first; you have not gone after young men... I will do for you all that you ask, for all the assembly of my people know that you are a worthy woman. But... there is another kinsman more closely related than I... if he will act as next-of-kin for you, good; let him do it. If he is not willing... then, as the Lord lives, I will act as next-of-kin.'

During the night, Ruth had done as Naomi instructed, 'uncovering the feet' of Boaz and then she laid down either at his feet or beside him (depending on the translation). When he stirred in the night, he realized that there was a woman next to him, but in the darkness could not recognize her. She identified herself, invited him to 'spread his cloak' over her (that is, take her into his bed) and explained that she was next of kin. She did so to claim that he was her *go'el*, her 'kinsman redeemer', with responsibility for her and her mother-in-law.

Boaz seemed pleased by her actions, which demonstrated her loyalty (presumably to Naomi) and her modesty, in choosing an older man rather than a young one. He would do everything she asked—that is, he would accept the role of *go'el*. However, there is a complication (the path of true love never runs smooth!) There is another relative with a prior claim on Ruth. Boaz says that he will ask him about it and, if he declines the responsibility, Boaz will happily do so. For the present, she should stay with him until the morning—which is much like saying, 'Let's burn our bridges behind us'!

Reflection

Ruth impressed the local people, who regarded her as a 'worthy' woman—quite an accolade for a Moabite immigrant!

DW

Right of redemption

No sooner had Boaz gone up to the gate and sat down there than the next-of-kin, of whom Boaz had spoken, came passing by. So Boaz said, 'Come over, friend; sit down here.'... Then Boaz took ten men of the elders of the city, and said, 'Sit down here'; so they sat down. He then said to the next-of-kin, 'Naomi... is selling the parcel of land that belonged to our kinsman Elimelech. So I thought I would tell you of it, and say: Buy it in the presence of those sitting here, and in the presence of the elders of my people. If you will redeem it, redeem it; but if you will not, tell me, so that I may know; for there is no one prior to you to redeem it, and I come after you.' So he said, 'I will redeem it.' Then Boaz said, 'The day you acquire the field... you are also acquiring Ruth the Moabite, the widow of the dead man, to maintain the dead man's name on his inheritance.' At this, the next-of-kin said, 'I cannot redeem it for myself without damaging my own inheritance. Take my right of redemption yourself.'

Redemption was a major feature of the social structure of the time. Land was kept in the family as much as possible, so, when a married man died, his nearest male relative was given first opportunity to buy it. He would 'redeem' it— that is, pay the price necessary to ensure its freedom from the ownership of others. That was the situation Boaz spelt out to Naomi's next-of-kin.

The man accepted his responsibility to redeem the land, but Boaz then pointed out that, if he did, part of the deal would be to take Ruth as his wife. The man, presumably already married with children, could see that this would mean that Ruth's children, not his own, would get his inheritance, so he declined. This seems to have been both what Boaz expected and wanted. It was probably also a relief to Ruth and Naomi, who had clearly set their sights on an alliance with Boaz rather than anyone else.

Reflection

Redemption is, of course, a great theme of the New Testament and the heart of the gospel. Jesus has 'paid the price' necessary to ensure our freedom from the 'ownership' of another. By redemption, we are his.

DW

Future blessing

Then Boaz said to the elders and all the people, 'Today you are witnesses that I have acquired from the hand of Naomi all that belonged to Elimelech and all that belonged to Chilion and Mahlon. I have also acquired Ruth the Moabite, the wife of Mahlon, to be my wife, to maintain the dead man's name on his inheritance, in order that the name of the dead may not be cut off from his kindred and from the gate of his native place; today you are witnesses.' Then all the people who were at the gate, along with the elders, said, 'We are witnesses. May the Lord make the woman who is coming into your house like Rachel and Leah, who together built up the house of Israel. May you produce children in Ephrathah and bestow a name in Bethlehem; and, through the children that the Lord will give you by this young woman, may your house be like the house of Perez, whom Tamar bore to Judah.'

While, as we have observed, in good stories the path of true love never runs smoothly, it is expected to reach its consummation in the end. Now, at last, Boaz is free to go public and declare not only that he will assume responsibility for Naomi and her family and land, but that he will take her Moabite daughter-in-law as his wife. The elders at the gate endorse his decision and add a formal blessing, likening Ruth to the 'mothers of Israel', Rachel and Leah, who also had connections with Bethlehem-Ephrathah (to give it its full name). They also invoked an ancestor of Boaz's, Perez, as a model of the new family, which would be blessed with many children.

This public approval was important, especially as the wife-to-be was a foreign immigrant. It says a lot about the open hearts of the people of Bethlehem, as expressed by their elders, that she could be so warmly welcomed. It also says much about Ruth, whose loyalty to Naomi, diligence in work and public assumption of the religion of Israel had been widely noted.

Reflection

Ruth made the decision to stay with Naomi and move to a foreign land without any promise of prosperity or marriage—as Naomi had frankly warned her. Now she would have both and the assurance of the community's approval and blessing.

DW

More to you than seven sons

So Boaz took Ruth and she became his wife. When they came together, the Lord made her conceive, and she bore a son. Then the women said to Naomi, 'Blessed be the Lord, who has not left you this day without next-of-kin; and may his name be renowned in Israel! He shall be to you a restorer of life and a nourisher of your old age; for your daughter-in-law who loves you, who is more to you than seven sons, has borne him.' Then Naomi took the child and laid him in her bosom, and became his nurse.

The women here act rather like the Chorus in a classical Greek play, their words providing an apt commentary on the events. Boaz married Ruth and, in due course, she bore him a son. The women's blessing expresses, in memorable language, the significance of this for Naomi. She had left Moab a destitute widow, without family and, hence, without support, but now, because of Boaz's commendable sense of duty, she has a son-in-law (a rich one at that) and a grandson. Yet, say the women, it is her daughter-in-law, Ruth, who is the key to it all—'more to you than seven sons'. That is some compliment in a society where it was sons that you needed for both prosperity and family honour.

The Lord had not left Naomi without kith and kin. Her family line will continue through the infant son who had been born to Ruth. Her sons' heritage has been preserved. If, as she had thought, the Lord had dealt harshly with her in the past, with the deaths of her husband and two sons, he has now seen fit to bless her in new and wonderful ways. Also, 'she became the child's nurse'—not his wet nurse, of course, but fulfilling her grandmotherly role of care and affection by sharing gladly in his upbringing. Some young mothers might have resented that, but the heart of Ruth is an open one (as the women say, Ruth 'loves you') and she probably sees it as a sign of the strength of the bond between them.

Reflection

The whole of this story—tragedy and blessing—is lived out 'under his wings', within the providence and care of the God of Israel.

DW

A royal line

The women of the neighbourhood gave him [the child] a name, saying, 'A son has been born to Naomi.' They named him Obed; he became the father of Jesse, the father of David. Now these are the descendants of Perez: Perez became the father of Hezron, Hezron of Ram, Ram of Amminadab, Amminadab of Nahshon, Nahshon of Salmon, Salmon of Boaz, Boaz of Obed, Obed of Jesse, and Jesse of David.

Like all good stories, the book of Ruth keeps the final twist in the plot right to the very end. We have followed the Moabite girl's journey from her homeland to Bethlehem, in touching loyalty to her bereaved and destitute mother-in-law. We have seen how she caught the attention of Naomi's rich kinsman, Boaz, and, through a daring stratagem, led him to accept—gladly, as it happened—his traditional responsibility to his kinswoman. We have been led through the subplot about the 'other' kinsman and then, it seems, finally, to the 'happy ever after' bit: Boaz and Ruth married and had a baby son, a grandchild for Naomi. The village chorus has sung its blessings. What more is there to say?

The answer is the stunning revelation in verse 17. We are given more clues in the genealogy that ends the book (all too easily ignored!) The ancestors of Boaz are descendants of Perez and you can read the amazing story of his conception and birth in Genesis 38. A precedent had been set for the 'irregular' introduction of Ruth, a Moabite, into this particular family tree. The women named the child of Ruth, Obed. He became the father of Jesse, who was the father of David. So, the great king of Israel, David, was not only a descendant of the aforementioned Perez but also the great-grandson of a Moabite immigrant. For Christians, there is a further thought here. Jesus, the Saviour of the world, therefore had an ancestor who was a member of the despised tribe of Moab—remember 'Moab is my washpot'? The Bible constantly throws these kinds of surprises at us.

Reflection

In the divine scheme of redemption, all nations and both genders have a part. Ruth is a reminder that God has no favourites. His salvation is as broad as his love and his love is as broad as his creation.

DW

Richard of Chichester

Here is a week of readings that we shall consider in relation to Richard of Chichester—the laughing, but hair-shirted, bishop who, appropriately, is best known now for one of his prayers. Richard (c. 1197–1253) is famous for being happy. He sounds like a Friar Tuck type—full of laughter and very hospitable. Many of the stories we have about him come from his friend and confessor, Friar Ralph Bocking. Friar Ralph describes how the people of Sussex, to whom Richard ministered, made a joke of his name, Ricardus—standing for 'RIdens, CARus, DUlcis', meaning 'laughing, beloved, sweet'.

This didn't mean that he was superficial. His good humour was bound up with his love of Jesus and his overwhelming sense of gratitude for what his redeemer and friend had done. This is reflected in his celebrated prayer:

Thanks be to thee, our Lord Jesus Christ, for all the benefits which thou hast given me, for all the pains and insults which thou hast borne for me. O most merciful Redeemer, Friend, and Brother, may I know thee more clearly, love thee more dearly, and follow thee more nearly. Amen

The first sentence of the prayer comes from Richard himself—words spoken on his deathbed. The rest was added later (probably in the early 20th century) to reflect his spirit and influence. The phrase 'day by day' seems to have been attached to the end even later.

It can seem disappointing that the prayer isn't all by the man himself, but I think it's important to be realistic about what has survived over so many centuries and grateful for one individual's continuing legacy.

Richard was born into a prosperous farming family in Droitwich, Worcestershire. He turned away from the family business to study at Oxford and later at Paris and Bologna. He became Chancellor of Oxford University—its head—and it wasn't until later that he became a priest. There was a dispute when he was made a bishop, as King Henry III preferred another candidate and refused to give him his lands or home at first (the Crown held the property when there was a vacancy). He was bishop for only eight years, but he made a huge impact. He was strict with his clergy, but also with himself, and cared greatly for the poor and sick.

Rachel Boulding

God's guiding hand in the wilderness

'If I go forward, he is not there; or backward, I cannot perceive him; on the left he hides, and I cannot behold him... But he knows the way that I take; when he has tested me, I shall come out like gold. My foot has held fast to his steps; I have kept his way and have not turned aside... For he will complete what he appoints for me.

It's far too easy with hindsight to see Richard's life as one of triumph as he was a firm but fair man, ministering to his flock, who loved him dearly. However, there were many times—including periods of whole years—when it wasn't like that. It must have seemed as if he would never get the chance even to begin his work properly when he spent two years at the beginning of his time as a bishop relying on handouts and hospitality as the king refused to give him his property.

Wouldn't it have felt to Richard as if God was hiding himself, as Job felt in this passage? We could understand if Richard felt lonely, isolated, even abandoned by God, but perhaps he was able to look back to an even bleaker experience in his life and see that God had not vanished, even if he couldn't feel the warm glow of his presence at that point. I'm thinking of the time in Richard's early life when he had to leave his studies at Oxford and return to help with the family farm after his father's death. This some-times happens in families. Often it is women who have to leave studying or paid work in order to keep the home going. Some have to cope with this all their lives. It might well have seemed as if he would never get the chance to have his own life, but Richard managed somehow to return to university and, eventually, become a priest. He trusted that God would complete what he had appointed for him, somehow (v. 14).

Reflection

We do not need to be very old to look back on life and see that things that we thought were disasters worked out to our good... we can see a guiding and a directing hand in it.

William Barclay (1907–78)

RB

God's love reaches beyond death

God has taken his stand in the council of heaven; in the midst of the gods he gives judgement: 'How long will you judge unjustly and show such favour to the wicked?... Rescue the weak and the poor; deliver them from the hand of the wicked'... Arise, O God and judge the earth, for it is you that shall take all nations for your possession.

Today is St Richard's Day, for it was on 16 June 1276 that his body was moved a few yards from a chapel at Chichester Cathedral to a shrine behind the high altar. He had been dead for 23 years at that point and was already recognized as a saint, so the new site became a place of pilgrimage. The fact that we celebrate Richard on this day rather than on the day of his birth, death or other significant event in his life reflects why he is important. He has had a life since his death that has mattered as much, if not more so, than anything he might have achieved in this world. He has a relationship with God that never ends. Such relationships in God's love are the sinews of the world.

This psalm above sets up a contrast between God's values and those of the world. The worldly gods are unjust and favour the wicked (v. 2), but the one true God is different: he wants to 'rescue the weak and the poor'. Richard was famed for his generosity to poor people—so much so that his financial advisers begged him to stop giving so much away as he was leaving nothing in the Church's resources. When he visited his flock, he would seek out the poor and sick, seeing them himself and giving them food.

The Old Testament constantly reminds us that God favours the needy and weak, yet we still need to recall this every day. We need to be told how the universe really functions—it is undergirded by God—as otherwise the worldly notions of 'every man for himself' creep in. That is why the habits of regular prayer, reading, reflection and worship are so important. They return us to the reality of God's rule.

Prayer

Father, help me to realize today that you take all nations for your possession (Psalm 82:8).

RB

Being content in plenty and in need

I have learned to be content with whatever I have. I know what it is to have little, and I know what it is to have plenty. In any and all circumstances I have learned the secret of being well-fed and of going hungry, of having plenty and of being in need. I can do all things through him who strengthens me.

Developing on yesterday's theme of God's values overturning those of the world, here is Paul thanking the Philippians for their support of his ministry. He is looking beyond the basic needs of survival and even the desire to have more than enough, searching for God's ideas of plenty.

Jesus never promises that his followers will be rich, but he does promise life in all its abundance (John 10:10). It reminds me of my favourite film, *I Know Where I'm Going*, released in 1945. In the Western Isles of Scotland, Joan (a stranger) observes to the local laird, 'People around here are very poor, I suppose.' He replies, 'Not poor, they just haven't got money.' 'It's the same thing', she argues. 'Oh, no, it's something quite different.' Among the many things that happen in the film, Joan comes to realize that cash isn't the answer to everything.

In a similar way, after he spent his first years as a bishop homeless and without money, Richard had to go from having absolutely no-thing, relying on others to feed and house him, to living in a bishop's palace and having enough to give away—even if his staff disapproved. Like Paul, he must have learnt the 'secret of… having plenty and of being in need'. It is reliance on God.

Such reliance isn't the idle irresponsibility of not working for your living and then expecting your family to survive on air, but the realization that feast or famine don't matter in themselves. If you are alive with just about enough to eat, the important thing is that all life is a wonderful gift from God, for which we should be grateful.

Reflection

Thank God, carefully and wonderingly, for your continuing privileges, and for every experience of his goodness. Thankfulness is a soil in which pride does not easily grow.

Archbishop Michael Ramsey (1904–88)

RB

Find rest unto your souls

At that time Jesus answered and said, 'I thank thee, O Father, Lord of heaven and earth, because thou hast hid these things from the wise and prudent, and hast revealed them unto babes... Come unto me, all ye that labour and are heavy laden, and I will give you rest. Take my yoke upon you, and learn of me; for I am meek and lowly in heart: and ye shall find rest unto your souls. For my yoke is easy, and my burden is light.'

This is the type of passage that might have given Richard the assurance he needed to defy the king. He realized that the king could, and did, deprive him of his home and possessions and could have done even worse than that. He wasn't anxious, though, because he knew that God was ultimately the one in control.

Richard saw the necessity of keeping to God's ways, not giving up in despair, even if others might have felt that God had abandoned him. Richard was known for spending hours in private prayer, opening himself up to God's will every day. Those who knew him reported that he would often get up very early, while the rest of the household (including his chaplains) was still asleep, and tiptoe to the chapel to pray before the business of the day began. He would tell himself off if the birds were already singing before he was up and praising God.

Such a quiet, regular habit, going on in an unshowy way, requires tremendous self-discipline to sustain, though, to someone looking in from outside, nothing much seems to be happening. Of course, it's this kind of steady, regular prayer, this daily offering to God, that provides the spiritual food needed to sustain us throughout the day. Without it, we are blown by every wind of circumstance and others' demands and have no sense of our own centre with God. It's when we know that we're loved and have taken the time to feel God's hand on our day that we can behave and respond in an honest way that reflects the truth of God in our lives.

Reflection

If we are to follow Christ, it must be in our common way of spending every day.

William Law (1686–1761),
A Serious Call to a Devout and Holy Life
RB

Jesus our loving friend and brother

This is my commandment, That ye love one another, as I have loved you. Greater love hath no man than this, that a man lay down his life for his friends. Ye are my friends, if ye do whatsoever I command you. Henceforth I call you not servants; for the servant knoweth not what his lord doeth: but I have called you friends; for all things that I have heard of my Father I have made known unto you... These things I command you, that ye love one another.

This passage is about a Lord who takes us into his confidence, who believes in us so much that he shares his insights and hopes with us. He makes us his friends.

It is appropriate for our reflections on Richard because of the following words from his famous prayer: 'O most merciful redeemer, friend and brother.' As we saw in the Introduction, these were added after he died, but were written in the spirit of his devotion. They seem to refer to the above Gospel passage, not just because they included the word 'friend' but also because of the ending of the prayer. Knowing Jesus more clearly relates to the contrast Jesus himself makes between a friend and a servant, who does not know what his Lord does. Loving him more dearly picks up on the main point of the passage (vv. 12, 17), that we love one another, while following more nearly corresponds to the whole idea of the intimacy of our relationships with friends.

One of the reasons for the special power the prayer has to move people is the way it places side by side our gratefulness to Jesus for the heart-stopping love he has shown us in bearing so much pain with the hope that this might spur us on in three specific areas, to which we can easily relate. We move from our gratitude on to our wish to know him more closely, which will lead inevitably to our loving him more. This, in turn, will enable us to follow him more closely. It's a simple progression that forms a journey of the heart: thankfulness to knowledge to love to follow-up in action. Jesus draws us into this, gently and lovingly, by inviting us to be his friends.

Reflection

The love and the thankfulness seem straightforward and easy enough, but what are you doing today to follow your friend Jesus more nearly?

RB

Lovest thou me?

So when they had dined, Jesus saith to Simon Peter, 'Simon, son of Jonas, lovest thou me more than these?' He saith unto him, 'Yea, Lord; thou knowest that I love thee.' He saith unto him, 'Feed my lambs.' He saith to him again the second time, 'Simon, son of Jonas, lovest thou me?' He saith unto him, 'Yea, Lord; thou knowest that I love thee.' He saith unto him, 'Feed my sheep.' He saith unto him the third time, 'Simon, son of Jonas, lovest thou me?' Peter was grieved because he said unto him the third time, 'Lovest thou me?'

This final passage, divided between today and tomorrow, shows Jesus after his resurrection, grilling Peter about what is going to happen next. Jesus isn't just asking if Peter really loves him, but what that love means—how much it will enable him to endure. Among other things, Jesus is saying that this love can't be merely a warm, cosy feeling or a sentimental gesture. This is a gift, but one that involves a hard, grown-up response: feeding the flock.

It is a fitting message in relation to Richard because of the way he combined the personal warmth and joy of love with a tough discipline. He was strict—most of all with himself, in that he dressed plainly, ate simply and didn't indulge in politics, gossip and ego trips (unlike many of his fellow bishops and, perhaps, even some bishops today). However, he could also demand nearly as much from others. He set high standards and even sacked those who flouted them by acting immorally and dishonestly. He dismissed one guilty priest, despite appeals from powerful people, including the king and queen, who could make life difficult for him.

It can seem hard (as it was for Peter here when he felt aggrieved that Jesus asked the same question three times) to connect the two faces of love—the affectionate generosity and the need to work at a mature response. However, they do belong together and each will gain from being part of a larger whole.

Reflection

Love is eager, sincere and kind; it is glad and lovely; it is strong, patient and faithful; wise, long-suffering and resolute; and it never seeks its own ends, for where a man seeks his own ends, he at once falls out of love.

Thomas à Kempis (c.1380–1471),
The Imitation of Christ
RB

What are you doing about this love?

And he [Peter] said unto him, 'Lord, thou knowest all things; thou knowest that I love thee.' Jesus saith unto him, 'Feed my sheep. Verily, verily, I say unto thee, When thou wast young, thou girdest thyself, and walkedst whither thou wouldest: but when thou shalt be old, thou shalt stretch forth thy hands, and another shall gird thee, and carry thee whither thou wouldest not.' This spake he, signifying by what death he should glorify God. And when he had spoken this, he saith unto him, 'Follow me.'

This second half of the passage we started to look at yesterday elaborates on the mature response to God's amazing love and tremendous gifts. Jesus describes how hard it will be to feed the flock. Also, his final words—'Follow me'—will take Peter to his own cross.

As we saw earlier, Jesus' words reflect the pattern of Richard's most famous prayer (see the Introduction to remind yourself of the full prayer). It starts with thankfulness to God for what he has done and leads, inevitably, through knowledge and love to our response of following Jesus. Yes, Jesus knows that we love him, but it's as if he looks us steadily in the eye and asks what we are going to do about it.

So, we have to keep asking ourselves this question, just as Jesus kept on asking Peter. Like Richard, we need to keep the laughter and the hard graft of discipline bound together, day by day. We can do this by means of regular prayer and active, generous concern for the needy, as Richard did. We know that God will sustain us when we do this consistently—even if it doesn't seem convenient or we don't feel like doing it.

We needn't feel disheartened that Richard is holier than us—the people who knew him didn't worry about that. Instead, we should recall and appreciate those qualities of warmth and closeness to God that made him both a saint and a greatly loved man who showed his friends the way to the Lord.

Reflection

'A saint is a human creature devoured and transformed by love: a love that has dissolved and burnt out those instinctive passions— acquisitive and combative, proud and greedy—which commonly rule the lives of men.'

Evelyn Underhill (1875–1941)
RB

Ecclesiastes—making sense of it all

It would be fair to say that the book of Ecclesiastes is not a particularly well-loved part of the Bible. It is not the place to turn to for a comforting thought for yourself or a friend. While there is the 'time for everything' passage and that nugget about 'eternity in the human heart', commentaries on Ecclesiastes tend to speak with one voice of 'existential despair' 'absurdity', 'futility', 'unrelieved gloom' and so on.

The *New Bible Commentary* (IVP, 1994) describes Ecclesiastes as the only biblical example of a style of writing that could be known as 'pessimism literature'. This genre belongs in the tradition of the Wisdom literature of the ancient Near East, going back to at least 2000BC. Interestingly, though, unlike such classics as *The Dialogue of Pessimism* (from 14th-century BC Babylonia, which advocates suicide as the only response to life's bleakness), Ecclesiastes also mentions the possibility of joy, faith and the assurance of God's goodness.

The book's date is uncertain, though some suggest the 5th century BC. The author is unknown, but, traditionally, is thought to be the ageing King Solomon, weary after a lifetime of wine, women and wealth. The speaker of the book is 'Teacher'—in Hebrew *Qoheleth*, rendered in Greek as *Ekklesiastes*, from which the book gets its name.

If we go with the idea that the book was written at some time around the high point of ancient Israel's power and riches, by somebody who had enjoyed at least some of the benefits of living in such a culture, we find uncannily contemporary echoes emerging as we read the text. Doesn't the Teacher sound just a bit like an Israelite Victor Meldrew, Mr Grumpy from the TV hit *One Foot in the Grave*? The difference here, though, is that the Teacher's complaints stem from a profound wisdom rather than an irritable personality. He is dissatisfied with easy answers to the deep questions with which he is wrestling and he wants us to dare to face them, too, without flinching.

Ecclesiastes is part of scripture because it challenges us to look beneath the surface of life and shows that we should not be afraid to do so. In the end, as the Teacher reminds us, God is still sovereign, even though we may sometimes lose a sense of his presence or his perspective on our little human affairs.

Naomi Starkey

Ecclesiastes 1:2–10 (TNIV, abridged)

A lot of hot air

'Meaningless! Meaningless!' says the Teacher. 'Utterly meaningless! Everything is meaningless!'... The sun rises and the sun sets, and hurries back to where it rises. The wind blows to the south and turns to the north; round and round it goes, ever returning on its course. All streams flow into the sea, yet the sea is never full... What has been will be again, what has been done will be done again; there is nothing new under the sun. Is there anything of which one can say, 'Look! This is something new'? It was here already, long ago; it was here before our time.

The Hebrew word for 'meaningless' originally meant 'breath' and has the sense of 'useless, pointless' (in King James' English, 'vanity of vanities'). We might say, 'It's a lot of hot air'. The Teacher is not just talking about empty words, however—for him, 'everything' is meaningless. Perhaps Mrs Teacher suggested a nice walk after a hard day's philosophy, but a stroll outdoors has simply added the natural world to his list of things he does not understand.

Elsewhere in scripture, creation is celebrated as being full of God's eternal presence and loving care. Compare the passage above with 'In the heavens [God] has pitched a tent for the sun, which is like a bridegroom coming out of his chamber, like a champion rejoicing to run his course' (Psalm 19:4–5). One observer sees meaningless repetition; another sees a burst of literal and metaphorical radiance. What consolation is there for the one who focuses not on the wonder but the undeniable monotony?

In *Orthodoxy* (1908), G.K. Chesterton suggests that only God is strong enough to bear the monotony of creation, delighting in it as a small child delights in repetition: 'It is possible that God says every morning, "Do it again" to the sun; and every evening, "Do it again" to the moon... It may be that He has the eternal appetite of infancy; for we have sinned and grown old, and our Father is younger than we.'

Jesus said, 'Unless you change and become like little children, you will never enter the kingdom of heaven' (Matthew 18:3). Perhaps we need to ask God to restore our sense of childlike wonder at the work of his hands (Psalm 19:1).

Reflection

Why do we tend to picture God as an old man?

NS

Empty pleasures

I said to myself, 'Come now, I will test you with pleasure to find out what is good.' But that also proved to be meaningless. 'Laughter,' I said, 'is madness. And what does pleasure accomplish?' I tried cheering myself with wine, and embracing folly—my mind still guiding me with wisdom. I wanted to see what was good for people to do under the heavens... I denied myself nothing my eyes desired; I refused my heart no pleasure. My heart took delight in all my labour... Yet when I surveyed all that my hands had done and what I had toiled to achieve, everything was meaningless.

The Teacher tries to cheer himself up by sampling a range of pleasures. His full list of activities (see vv. 4–9) reads a bit like the advice routinely doled out to the downcast and stressed by agony aunts today: go for a drink with friends, have a laugh, contact a dating agency, get a cleaner, try retail therapy, gardening, improving your finances...

He admits that he enjoys the general busyness, but, when he steps back to survey the result, the clouds have not lifted and he asks, 'Just what exactly was the point of that?' This is a question that we are not encouraged to ask by the market forces that drive so much of our culture. The possibility that 'more' does not automatically equal 'better' or 'happier' is, in many ways, dangerously subversive.

A Polish man was in the news last year for waking from a 19-year coma to find his country transformed. Jan Grzebski remembered a communist country with nothing in the shops but tea and vinegar, long petrol queues and meat rationing. Now, Poland is a democracy and a member of the EU and consumer goods are everywhere. Still, he was amazed at 'all these people who walk around with their mobile phones and never stop moaning'.

We would do well to pause and ponder the Teacher's experiences before embarking on the next scheme or purchase that will (we hope) make all the difference to our lives. Let's dare to ask ourselves the question, 'Just what exactly is the point of that?'

Reflection

Jesus enjoyed eating, drinking and the company of friends, but emphasized that such pleasures should not be our chief objective: 'Seek first [God's] kingdom and his righteousness' (Matthew 6:33).

NS

Why bother working?

So my heart began to despair over all my toilsome labour under the sun. For people may labour with wisdom, knowledge and skill, and then they must leave all they own to others who have not toiled for it. This too is meaningless and a great misfortune. What do people get for all the toil and anxious striving with which they labour under the sun? All their days their work is grief and pain; even at night their minds do not rest. This too is meaningless.

It has to be said, teenagers do existential angst very well. For many people, life is never quite so bleak as it is when you are 16—until you get to be a Grumpy Old Man like the Teacher (or even Woman), that is.

The passage above reads a bit like the kind of lament many parents have to endure from teenage children during the school exam season: 'OK, so I revise for these exams. For what? The chance to take harder exams next year and the year after and the year after that, then go out to work and get a mortgage and slave away until I am too old to enjoy myself? Will somebody please explain why I should bother?' Their parents lie awake at night, worrying about what they must have done wrong for their children to have such negative attitudes.

Yet, like the issue of whether or not material goods and pleasures really can lead to fulfilment, it is worth reflecting on the implications of the Teacher's words. While a fair number of people may choose to not make financial comfort their sole aim in life, the importance of getting a good—indeed, 'the best' —education is rarely questioned. In many parts of the UK (and no doubt elsewhere), family life is dominated by getting children into the 'best' school or university. You don't often hear of 'good enough' being sufficient.

Once again, with the Teacher, let's revisit that assumption. Are we unthinkingly training our children/godchildren/grandchildren in the ways of 'toil and anxious striving' or do we manage to step back and try to discern a bigger picture? Are we truly open to hearing God's guidance on this and other practical matters or do we assume that he cares as much about school league tables as we do?

Prayer

Lord, give us the grace to glimpse our lives from your perspective.

NS

A time for everything

There is… a season for every activity under the heavens: a time to be born and a time to die, a time to plant and a time to uproot, a time to kill and a time to heal… a time to weep and a time to laugh, a time to mourn and a time to dance… a time to embrace and a time to refrain, a time to search and a time to give up, a time to keep and a time to throw away… a time to be silent and a time to speak, a time to love and a time to hate, a time for war and a time for peace.

Some may be surprised to find these verses in the Bible. Hands up those of you whose first thought was, 'Surely that was a hit by The Byrds?' In fact the Teacher got there first, followed eventually by folk singer Pete Seeger, who wrote 'Turn, Turn, Turn'.

What is striking about this famous passage is how positive and negative appear to balance each other, the pendulum of life swinging from one to the other with neither being given more weight than the other. The implication is twofold. First, even when we think positively, circumstances may not develop as we might hope. Second, the fear of darkness without end is shown to be unfounded. The repetitiveness of each day, which so depressed the Teacher, offers the hope of a new start, of new possibilities.

Steve Griffiths' book *God of the Valley* (BRF, 2003) interweaves Bible reflections on grief with his own experience of loss when his wife died after a long illness, aged 36. He tells of how he came to make a conscious decision to move on from defining himself in terms of bereavement: 'This was not to deny my past; it was a question of forming a healthy identity that could undergird my healing.'

There is a time to mourn, to weep, to uproot, but there is also a time for dancing, laughing, planting. We may feel that we do not have the strength to move from the negative to the positive (or vice versa), yet we can ask our heavenly Father by his Spirit to help us embrace the next stage of our journey, wherever it may take us.

Reflection

The Lord will watch over your coming and going both now and for evermore (Psalm 121:8).

NS

God is sovereign

He [God] has made everything beautiful in its time. He has also set eternity in the human heart; yet no one can fathom what God has done from beginning to end. I know that there is nothing better for people than to be happy and to do good while they live. That each of them may eat and drink, and find satisfaction in all their toil—this is the gift of God. I know that everything God does will endure forever; nothing can be added to it and nothing taken from it.

This is one of those lyrical passages that grace even the bleakest books of the Bible. In its contrast with much of what surrounds it, there are resonances of Lamentations 3:22–24 (the 'great is your faithfulness' bit) and Job 19:25–27 (the 'I know that my redeemer lives' bit).

What causes this apparent change of heart? There are probably many scholarly arguments and genre-related reasons, but, just possibly, it may have happened a bit like this. Mrs Teacher comes home from a hard day selling olives at the local market and visiting her sister. She has kept the peace between four children, haggled for a new water jar and dealt with a lame donkey. She finds the Teacher in the same position as when she left that morning, still moodily poking the ashes of the fire and brooding about universal futility.

Holding her tongue (for she is a wise woman), Mrs Teacher hands him the baby to mind and sends him out into the cool of the day while she prepares a meal. He leans against a wall and the baby gurgles in his arms, while the moon rises slowly over the hill and a nightingale starts singing somewhere in the growing dusk.

Then the Teacher's heart is filled with gratitude and his eyes are opened to the goodness and beauty of the world. At last, he gives thanks.

Yesterday, we saw that, in our temporally confined cosmos, there is a time for everything, both good and bad. Today, we are reminded that this life, this planet—and the farthest reaches of the farthest galaxies—are not all there is. In the beginning, God made it very good, yet our hearts tell us that one day it will be even better, world without end.

Reflection

What has given you a glimpse of eternity?

NS

ECCLESIASTES 4:8–12 (TNIV)

Two are better than one

There was a man all alone; he had neither son nor brother. There was no end to his toil, yet his eyes were not content with his wealth. 'For whom am I toiling,' he asked, 'and why am I depriving myself of enjoyment?'... Two are better than one, because they have a good return for their labour: if they fall down, they can help each other up... Also, if two lie down together, they will keep warm. But how can one keep warm alone? Though one may be overpowered, two can defend themselves. A cord of three strands is not quickly broken.

This passage points out the practical advantages of companionship when contrasted with the 'man all alone'. In a culture built around the extended family, to have 'neither son nor brother' was to be at enormous economic and social disadvantage. The man's hard-earned wealth became truly pointless without heirs with whom to share it and there was no possibility of 'leaving it all to a good cause'.

While the verses about 'two are better than one' are used in marriage services from time to time, they are applicable to far more situations than that. Unlike the ancient world (and some parts of the world today), modern Western culture tends to idolize the individual, especially the one who asserts him- or herself against an oppressive 'system'. To be described as 'strong', 'independent', 'self-realized' and so on is seen as entirely positive, but not so many would like to be told that they are 'needy', 'codependent' or 'unassertive'.

Whether we live in a traditional family unit, alone or an extended household, though, we do need other people. Even those of us who do not relish crowds or are so happy being solitary that we can go for days without speaking to another person, each of us has a network, large or small, of human relationships that surrounds and— all being well—supports us.

Interestingly, people are often drawn to their local church by a desire to be 'part of the community'. Faith issues may be way down their agenda to start with, but the simple wish to belong can become a keyhole through which God's love can shine.

Prayer

Father God, we pray for any who are lonely. May you bring companionship into their lives.

NS

A meaningful life

A man may have a hundred children and live many years; yet no matter how long he lives, if he cannot enjoy his prosperity and does not receive proper burial, I say that a stillborn child is better off than he. It comes without meaning, it departs in darkness, and in darkness its name is shrouded. Though it never saw the sun or knew anything, it has more rest than does that man—even if he lives a thousand years twice over but fails to enjoy his prosperity. Do not all go to the same place?

Here, two lives are contrasted. First, we hear of a rich man, blessed with personal longevity and also fecundity—a very different situation from yesterday's 'man all alone'. His life is troubled, though, and, when it eventually draws to a close, it sounds as if none of his many children cared enough to give him proper funeral honours. Rather than enjoying his wealth, he may have hoarded it 'where moth and rust destroy' (Matthew 6:19), worried that he never really had enough.

Then there is the story of a baby who had an 'untimely birth' (v. 3, KJV), which could suggest premature birth as well as the 'stillborn' of modern translations. The phrase 'comes without meaning' is the same as the 'meaningless/vanity/hot air' sentiment expressed at the very start of the book. More poignantly, we could think of the child's life being as brief as a 'puff of air'. It did not live long enough to be named. We are not even told its sex.

The lesson drawn from the comparison is shocking—that the dead baby is better off than the old man because at least the infant has 'more rest'. The underlying challenge, however, is whether or not we make best use of the time with which we have been blessed. Will our lives be marked by cruelty, selfishness, indifference? Will we leave friends and family—even the earth itself—bruised by our presence? Contrast that with the faint imprint that accompanies the child's passing.

These days even the tiniest of babies who die are named, mourned and remembered with love. Even if they never drew breath, they are considered unique beings, unrepeatable combinations of DNA. Like them, each one of us is a miracle of God's hand, our lives a privilege to squander or treasure as we choose.

Reflection

How might people remember you?

NS

ECCLESIASTES 7:10–12; 8:1 (TNIV)

The good old days?

Do not say, 'Why were the old days better than these?' For it is not wise to ask such questions. Wisdom, like an inheritance, is a good thing and benefits those who see the sun. Wisdom is a shelter as money is a shelter, but the advantage of knowledge is this: wisdom preserves the life of its possessor… Who is like the wise? Who knows the explanation of things? Wisdom brightens the face and changes its hard appearance.

Nostalgia is not a new problem—and 'problem' it can certainly be! While it is undoubtedly good to have a sense of where we have come from, both individually and as communities, a problem can develop when we allow ourselves to long for a past that may be more imagination than reality. When that happens, cherished memories of places, persons or events can end up blighting what God is trying to do in and through us in the present.

Equally unhelpfully, some people can dwell on past hurts obsessively so that they become unable to believe anything good has ever happened to them. The darkness in their past overshadows all that has taken place since then, so they find God's blessings hard to discern.

The Teacher keeps returning to the question, 'What is the point of life?' He highlights the folly of swallowing whole our society's values and offering superficially easy answers to profound questions. The point of life, the Teacher reminds

us, is becoming wise. It is not wise to spend our days lamenting the past when life seemed better. Cultivating a wise heart can involve facing squarely the times when life was bad, but then choosing to seek God's healing and help to move forward into a positive future.

The verses above describe some extremely practical benefits of wisdom: a comfortable existence and a healthy, long-lived one. The wise know 'the explanation of things'— 'how' and 'why', rather than just 'what'. Oh, and as the final verse points out, wisdom performs as efficiently, if not more so, than any expensive moisturizer on the face.

How do we get hold of this wonderful product? Ask God, 'who gives generously to all without finding fault, and it will be given' (see James 1:5).

Prayer

Generous God, please touch us with something of your wisdom.

NS

Zero tolerance

When the sentence for a crime is not quickly carried out, people's hearts are filled with schemes to do wrong. Although a wicked person who commits a hundred crimes may live a long time, I know that it will go better with those who fear God, who are reverent before him. Yet because the wicked do not fear God, it will not go well with them, and their days will not lengthen like a shadow. There is something else meaningless that occurs on earth: the righteous who get what the wicked deserve, and the wicked who get what the righteous deserve.

This passage is a disturbing picture of what happens when communities go into meltdown, when a society's values no longer seem to be understood or affirmed. Ancient Israel was founded on the laws of God and a look almost anywhere else in the Old Testament shows how clearly rewards and punishments were laid out for those who kept—or broke—those laws. So it did indeed seem 'meaningless' when the Teacher saw the reward due to the righteous apparently going to benefit the wicked.

I say 'apparently' because, as the Teacher points out, in the end, wilfully breaking God's laws does not lead to a life of *shalom*—the wonderful Hebrew word that refers to prosperity, well-being, safety, fulfilment and so on. Once again, we are called to look at the bigger picture, seeing how the bitter fruit of selfishness, cruelty and greed can emerge over a number of generations instead of envying one group or individual's short-term power, wealth and success.

What we are also called to do is ensure that society upholds the rule of law. The concept of 'zero tolerance policing' asserts that if minor transgressions are unchecked (graffiti, public drunkenness, vandalism and so on), then more serious crime will start to flourish. While that approach is not without its critics, it remains the case that Christians should be at the forefront of caring for their communities and working with others (whether or not they share a common faith) to bring about changes that echo the values of the kingdom of God.

Reflection

Blessed are those who do not walk in step with the wicked… They are like a tree planted by steams of water, which yields its fruit in season (Psalm 1:1, 3).

NS

Enjoy what you can

Go, eat your food with gladness, and drink your wine with a joyful heart, for God has already approved what you do. Always be clothed in white, and always anoint your head with oil. Enjoy life with your wife, whom you love, all the days of this meaningless life that God has given you under the sun—all your meaningless days. For this is your lot in life and in your toilsome labour under the sun. Whatever your hand finds to do, do it with all your might, for in the realm of the dead, where you are going, there is neither working nor planning nor knowledge nor wisdom.

Things start off well here—the Teacher seems to have moved on from asking awkward questions and pointing out painful truths to celebrating the good life that God has bestowed on us. Then it all seems to go horribly wrong, like one of those nightmare best man's speeches, where the guests start off smiling and then fall silent, squirming in their seats as the soon-to-be-former friend dredges up one embarrassing fact after another.

Why does the Teacher do a similar thing here? Why endorse dressing well, high standards of personal grooming and a strong work ethic if the whole business is actually 'meaningless'? I think this is actually the Teacher's shock tactics again, just as when he stated that the stillborn baby had had a better life than the rich man who died friendless.

Once again, we are confronted with the uncomfortable message that we should not rate this existence too highly—it is fleeting, a mere breath of wind in the great scheme of things. At the same time, we are warned to value the little space that we have been given. We should live in a spirit of gratitude, enjoying that which has been granted us to enjoy. Those who have faced death sometimes speak of a similar paradox—seeing how small life is, yet how wonderful.

Yes, we will all die one day—wise and foolish, righteous and wicked alike. Unlike the Teacher, though, we of the new covenant know that there is hope beyond the grave. We will sleep, but then we will be raised to a new life for which our years here have been just a preparation.

Reflection

Before you eat your main meal today, offer thanks to the Giver and then eat with gladness.

NS

Poor but wise

There was once a small city with only a few people in it. And a powerful king came against it, surrounded it and built huge siege works against it. Now there lived in that city a man poor but wise, and he saved the city by his wisdom. But nobody remembered that poor man. So I said, 'Wisdom is better than strength.' But the poor man's wisdom is despised, and his words are no longer heeded. The quiet words of the wise are more to be heeded than the shouts of a ruler of fools. Wisdom is better than weapons of war, but one sinner destroys much good.

The Teacher presents us with another story and it has been suggested that perhaps here he might have been speaking from his own experience. Maybe he was the man, 'poor but wise', whose efforts secured the defeat of the massive forces ranged against his people. When the victory celebrations were in full flow, however, nobody even remembered what he had done, let alone organized a public tribute. His only reward was that he knew what good he had done—and for a truly wise man perhaps that was enough.

Even though wisdom's voice is quiet, it is still effective—provided that somebody else listens. The translation of these verses is not straightforward. Apparently they could be rendered as meaning that nobody took any notice of the poor man's quiet, wise words so the city was not saved after all and the bawling of a bullying regime drowned out any whisper about following a different way.

The final verse above underlines the difficulties of the path trod by peacemakers, then as now. Throughout history, those who make war grab the headlines and a victory through force of arms is written up as heroic, whether in digital, pen and ink or stone column form. Making peace is an altogether less glamorous affair—it requires endless patience, tact and a willingness to go back and forth until all are in agreement. People are less likely to write poems or paint scenes of long, drawn-out negotiations around conference tables, yet that is the way of wisdom according to this passage.

Prayer

Lord Jesus, help us to remember that in your Kingdom it is the poor, the meek and the peacemakers who are singled out for blessing.

NS

Taking risks

Ship your grain across the sea; after many days you may receive a return. Invest in seven ventures, yes, in eight; you do not know what disaster may come upon the land. If clouds are full of water, they pour rain on the earth. Whether a tree falls to the south or to the north, in the place where it falls, there it will lie. Whoever watches the wind will not plant; whoever looks at the clouds will not reap... Sow your seed in the morning, and at evening let your hands not be idle, for you do not know which will succeed, whether this or that, or whether both will do equally well.

The traditional translation of the opening verse is, in my opinion, rather unhelpfully literal: 'cast your bread upon the waters'. Before I was old enough to know better, it conjured up images of feeding ducks in the park. What could possibly be the return for that—wild duck à l'orange?

In fact, the Teacher is giving economic and trading advice here. It's another variation on the theme in Ecclesiastes of making the most of what we have, which is echoed elsewhere in the Bible—Jesus' parable of the talents, for example (Matthew 25:14–30). The servant who hid his money in the ground would have benefited from the Teacher's bracing words: 'stop dithering, checking the forecasts and worrying about the best time to invest. Be bold! Take calculated risks and it will (probably) go well for you.'

These biblical business principles assume, however, that the hearers have been working away at acquiring one vital asset—wisdom. The Teacher is not suggesting that we cash in our worldly goods and blow the lot on lottery tickets. He is no advocate of recklessness—a characteristic of the proverbial fool—but, to those who are hesitating about embarking on a new venture in case it goes pear-shaped, he prescribes a combination of decisiveness, shrewdness and prudence. Rather than lying around, dreaming of a better life, we should be prepared to work for it, but work wisely.

Reflection

Eat honey, my son, for it is good; honey from the comb is sweet to your taste. Know also that wisdom is like honey for you: if you find it, there is a future hope for you, and your hope will not be cut off (Proverbs 24:13–14).

NS

Advice for the youth

Remember your Creator in the days of your youth, before the days of trouble come and the years approach when you will say, 'I find no pleasure in them'—before the sun and the light and the moon and the stars grow dark, and the clouds return after the rain... Remember him—before the silver cord is severed, and the golden bowl is broken; before the pitcher is shattered at the spring, and the wheel broken at the well, and the dust returns to the ground it came from, and the spirit returns to God who gave it.

The richness of the poetic imagery here (do also read verses 2–5) makes the text difficult to translate with certainty, but many commentators feel that the references to gathering clouds, darkness and so on could be referring to the physical limitations of old age (failing sight, weak limbs, silver hair and so on). Even if they are not so specific, they give a vivid impression of desolation and decay.

The Teacher is warning people to not ignore their relationship with God until 'the days of trouble come', whether that coincides with literal old age or not. Rather than searching for the Lord in a hurry, driven by circumstances, he asks that we consider making that search our life's priority from the earliest days. Otherwise, we may start too late and find that time has run out—the cord will have been severed, the bowl broken, the pitcher and wheel shattered—and we will find ourselves face to face with the living God having barely begun to make his acquaintance.

There is a challenge here, then, for the Church, which is that it continue to make every effort to reach out to younger people. Those in their 20s and 30s are often the missing generation in many congregations. While some return with their own children in later years (perhaps to secure a place at the local church school), many become so busy with work, family and leisure commitments that 'going to church' never features. The Church needs the young, their energy, enthusiasm and sense of boundless possibility. As for the young, they need to remember their Creator.

Reflection

Seek the Lord while he may be found; call on him while he is near (Isaiah 55:6).

NS

In conclusion

Not only was the Teacher wise, but also he imparted knowledge to the people. He pondered and searched out and set in order many proverbs... The words of the wise are like goads, their collected sayings like firmly embedded nails—given by one shepherd. Be warned, my son, of anything in addition to them. Of making many books there is no end, and much study wearies the body. Now all has been heard; here is the conclusion of the matter: fear God and keep his commandments, for this is the duty of every human being. For God will bring every deed into judgment, including every hidden thing, whether it is good or evil.

Some commentators think that these concluding verses are a later addition, an attempt to reconcile the jagged, uncomfortable message of Ecclesiastes with the rest of scripture. Others argue that, throughout the book, there are reminders that, however empty life seems, there is a wider perspective on it all—that of the Creator God.

Admitting that there are unanswerable questions and spells of despondency on the discipleship road is not the same as turning aside from that road and rejecting belief altogether. Interestingly, in Jewish tradition Ecclesiastes is read each year (during the autumnal Festival of Booths). We might do well to establish a similar practice, if only to confound those who accuse Christians of peddling a shallow faith with a glib answer or proof text for every situation.

We may speculate on whether or not it was the Teacher's scribe leaving us a portrait of the wise and, by now, probably old man with a firm reminder of just how hard he worked, in case (then as now) some were inclined to dismiss philosophy as a waste of time. The Teacher's words may challenge and exasperate us in equal measure, but we need such probing, prophetic voices to keep us from complacency and from the temptation to push hard issues to the margins of life.

We can also muse on the possibility that the Teacher—whether King Solomon or an unknown other—is now in the presence of God, finally finding out the answers to all his conundrums.

Prayer

Thank you, Father, for the certain hope that one day we will talk with you face to face—and understand.

NS

The 'I am' sayings of Jesus

All down the ages, multitudes of Christians have argued and analysed, pondered and philosophized about just who this man is, a man who lived and died in the Middle East two millennia ago and whose Spirit continues to flow through the river of humanity today, bringing life wherever it flows and carrying each of us to our destiny in the bottomless ocean of God's love.

Jesus' own contemporaries asked him, 'Who are you? Are you the one we are waiting for?' (see, for example, Luke 7:18), but Jesus doesn't offer any neat definitions. He doesn't carry an ID card. He doesn't need to. He is who he is and in this truth lies the echo of God's words to Moses, from the heart of the burning bush: 'I am who I am' (Exodus 3:13–15). He is being—simple, total and perfect being.

Any name we might come up with to define the mystery of God is going to fall far short of the truth. The language of logic and reason will always let us down, but the language of image and metaphor is more helpful. In his 'I am' sayings, Jesus tries to break through the limitations of human language and thought patterns, describing to his friends some ways in which they might come closer to grasping something of his identity.

• I'm like a gate, a way of passing through the boundaries of your understanding to encounter the source of your being.
• I'm like a shepherd who knows and cares for you more deeply than you know or care for yourself.
• I'm like a light, with the power to lighten your darkest corners and bring hope to your darkest hours.
• I'm like bread, nourishing your eternal reality and enabling you to grow into the fullness of all you can be.
• I'm not a map for your journey, but I'm the journey itself, revealing my truth to you in every step, living my life in you with every breath.
• I'm the one who gives you life and sustains your being as surely as the vine produces the grape and holds it in being.
• I'm the growth through all your diminishments, the new beginning beyond all your endings.

The amazing thing is that, when we allow ourselves to be drawn into the mystery of who Jesus is, he leads us more and more fully into the mystery of who we are ourselves and all we are called to become.

Margaret Silf

JOHN 10:1–5, 7, 9–10 (NRSV, ABRIDGED)

I am the gate

'Very truly, I tell you, anyone who does not enter the sheepfold by the gate but climbs in by another way is a thief and a bandit. The one who enters by the gate is the shepherd of the sheep. The gate-keeper opens the gate for him, and the sheep hear his voice. He calls his own sheep by name and leads them out. When he has brought out all his own, he goes ahead of them, and the sheep follow him because they know his voice. They will not follow a stranger, but they will run from him because they do not know the voice of strangers.'… So again Jesus said to them, 'Very truly, I tell you, I am the gate for the sheep… I am the gate. Whoever enters by me will be saved, and will come in and go out and find pasture. The thief comes only to steal and kill and destroy. I came that they may have life and have it abundantly.'

Do you remember learning about magnetism at school, using a piece of paper, some iron filings and a magnet? Do you remember how the filings responded to the magnet's pull, like living particles, dancing to the music of attraction?

All this came back to me recently when we installed a cat flap, which is operated by a magnet on the cats' collars. Our two cats soon realized that the flap would open when they pushed their noses against it. Suddenly a whole new world of freedom has opened up to them, but they always come home to be fed and loved. They know where they belong.

God's love is a magnet stronger than anything we can imagine, calling us to abundant life in him.

Our own hearts, where God is indwelling, are like those iron filings, living particles of love in the core of our being, invited to respond to God's desire to draw us to himself. Like the cats, we know, deep down, where we belong. We know the voice that calls us, the heart that loves us and the one who is our gateway to that love.

Prayer

O God, draw us to yourself, for we have no home except in you. Give us the trust and courage to enter by the gate you have given us.

MS

Come home to me

'Ask, and it will be given to you; search, and you will find; knock, and the door will be opened for you. For everyone who asks receives, and everyone who searches finds, and for everyone who knocks, the door will be opened... Enter through the narrow gate; for the gate is wide and the road is easy that leads to destruction, and there are many who take it. For the gate is narrow and the road is hard that leads to life, and there are few who find it.'

One of our cats, Hoppy, has only three legs, so is slightly less agile than the other, Jasper. Jasper is a bit of a scatterbrain. It took them a while to get used to the cat flap. Hoppy needed a little ramp to enable him to reach up to the flap. Jasper needed to have his nose nudged into it a few times before he got the message. Once they had learned how the flap worked, they still had to go through the narrow tunnel between the big wide world and the loving home that awaited them. We watched, with a smile, their initial apprehension and then their growing confidence that this gateway would indeed open at their touch.

Jesus didn't say that it would be easy to enter through the gate. First, like the cats, we have to want to come in. The magnet of love will do the rest, but we still have to entrust ourselves to the narrow path. That takes courage.

Like Hoppy, we may need a ramp to bring us closer to the gate.

Perhaps you remember with gratitude who or what has helped you personally to come closer to Jesus the gate. You may be like Jasper and need a few lessons before you get the message. Has anyone helped you to grasp the truth that Jesus does indeed open the Kingdom to us?

The main motivator for the cats, however, is the sheer desire to get into their warm and welcoming home. If they are so attracted to the place where they belong, how much greater is our attraction to where we belong—the very heart of God?

Reflection

May we trust that the tunnel of our life's journey is truly towards love.

MS

John 10:11–17 (NRSV)

I am the good shepherd

'I am the good shepherd. The good shepherd lays down his life for the sheep. The hired hand, who is not the shepherd and does not own the sheep, sees the wolf coming and leaves the sheep and runs away—and the wolf snatches them and scatters them. The hired hand runs away because a hired hand does not care for the sheep. I am the good shepherd. I know my own and my own know me, just as the Father knows me and I know the Father. And I lay down my life for the sheep. I have other sheep that do not belong to this fold. I must bring them also, and they will listen to my voice. So there will be one flock, one shepherd. For this reason the Father loves me, because I lay down my life in order to take it up again.'

A story is told about a servant who was asked by his master to build a house. The servant thought that this would be a good opportunity to make some money on the side, so he skimped on all the building materials, cutting corners wherever he possibly could. Imagine his dismay when the master made a gift to him of the finished house. 'Had I known it was for me, I would have given it my very best', he reflected ruefully, as he moved into the shoddy house.

When Jesus reveals himself as 'the good shepherd', he shows us, among other things, what it means to accept the responsibility of ownership. Even we mortals know that we will take good care of what we own, although we may be less careful with things that don't belong to us. Jesus goes much further. He reveals the cost of owner-

ship. He knows his own and, like a devoted shepherd, he will defend us to the death. We know just how costly that death was and what an eternity of selfless loving it would open up to all who follow the shepherd's call, including those who don't yet know that they belong to the fold and still haven't heard the shepherd's voice.

Reflection

The wolf snatches and scatters. The shepherd calls and gathers. May we always have the grace to know the difference.

MS

MATTHEW 18:2–4, 10–14 (NRSV)

Live in my care

He [Jesus] called a child, whom he put among them, and said, 'Truly I tell you, unless you change and become like children, you will never enter the kingdom of heaven. Whoever becomes humble like this child is the greatest in the kingdom of heaven... Take care that you do not despise one of these little ones; for I tell you, in heaven their angels continually see the face of my Father in heaven. What do you think? If a shepherd has a hundred sheep, and one of them has gone astray, does he not leave the ninety-nine on the mountains and go in search of the one that went astray? And if he finds it, truly I tell you, he rejoices over it more than over the ninety-nine that never went astray. So it is not the will of your Father in heaven that one of these little ones should be lost.'

Jesus the good shepherd shows us the difference between owning something, caring for it for its own sake, and merely possessing something for the sake of what we can gain from it. Equally, there is a huge difference between being owned and being merely possessed. The shepherd to whom we truly belong will cherish us. The wolf, who possesses us by force, will devour us. The 'wolf' takes many forms, sometimes coming at us in the shape of the exaggerated fears and disordered desires that too often dominate our hearts.

Whatever shape our wolves may take, Jesus reminds us that we belong, eternally, to God, the source of our being, and holds out to us this promise of God's protection against the wolves. How do we claim that protection? With the characteristic simplicity of the Kingdom, Jesus chooses a little child to teach us. He invites us simply to live in the care of the one to whom we belong, as trustingly as a little child entrusts himself to his parents' arms.

To belong to the shepherd is to be in a real, living relationship with him and accept his invitation to live in his care. He won't take 'no' for an answer—he will keep on searching, calling and inviting until we respond.

Reflection
True freedom lies not in going our own ways, but in belonging to the One who is infinitely greater than ourselves.

MS

I am the light of the world

Again Jesus spoke to them, saying, 'I am the light of the world. Whoever follows me will never walk in darkness but will have the light of life.'... Jesus said to them, 'The light is with you for a little longer. Walk while you have the light, so that the darkness may not overtake you. If you walk in the darkness, you do not know where you are going. While you have the light, believe in the light, so that you may become children of light.' ... Then Jesus cried aloud: 'Whoever believes in me believes not in me but in him who sent me... I have come as light into the world, so that everyone who believes in me should not remain in the darkness. I do not judge anyone who hears my words and does not keep them, for I came not to judge the world, but to save the world.'

Imagine a long-distance truck driver. He's still learning the ropes. It's his first journey with the vehicle and night has fallen. Ahead of him are hundreds of miles of deep, dense darkness and he can see absolutely nothing. He switches on his engine, full of fears about the road ahead. In the headlights' gleam, he can see about 100 metres of the road, but what are 100 metres of light compared with hundreds of miles of darkness?

'It's no use!' he says to himself. 'In just a few metres I shall be out of the light and into the pitch darkness.' And so, perhaps, he pulls on the brake and settles down in his little patch of light, so great are his fears of the dark.

But perhaps he decides to drive forward in the little light he has. If so, he will, of course, discover that the light travels with him, always illuminating the next section of road in front of him.

What about you? Do you fear the darkness more than you trust the light or can you trust that the light will always be there ahead of you, guiding your next steps?

Reflection

To discover the continuing presence of the light, we have to risk walking towards the darkness. We call this trust 'faith'.

MS

Let your light shine

In the beginning was the Word, and the Word was with God, and the Word was God. He was in the beginning with God. All things came into being through him, and without him not one thing came into being. What has come into being in him was life, and the life was the light of all people. The light shines in the darkness, and the darkness did not overcome it. There was a man sent from God, whose name was John. He came as a witness to testify to the light, so that all might believe through him. He himself was not the light, but he came to testify to the light. The true light, which enlightens everyone, was coming into the world.

A friend once pointed out to me something that is abundantly obvious, yet it startled me with its simple truth. You can easily try the experiment for yourself.

Wait for a dark night. Inside your home, the lights are on. Now, open the door to the outside world. What happens? Does the darkness come into your home or does the light from your home go out into the darkness, actually dispelling the darkness?

No prizes for getting the answer right, yet what is so obvious in daily life can become so difficult in the life of faith. Jesus declares himself to be the light of the world. Why, then, are we so afraid of the darkness?

Now try a different experiment. Reflect on any problem that you are trying to deal with in your life right now. Take a long hard look at it and notice especially any areas of darkness. Now go deep into the core of your being and listen to Jesus' words: 'I am the light of the world'. You carry that light within you, just as John did. You are not yourself that light, but your life is a carrier of the light in a way that is unique to you alone.

What happens to your problem now? Does its darkness invade the core of your being or does the light at the heart of you spill out and dispel it?

Reflection

May the light that God has kindled in each of our hearts spill freely out into the darkest corners of our lives and our world.

MS

I am the bread of life

[Jesus said] 'Do not work for food that perishes, but for the food that endures for eternal life, which the Son of Man will give you.'... So they [the crowd] said to him, 'What sign are you going to give us then, so that we may see it and believe you? What work are you performing? Our ancestors ate the manna in the wilderness; as it is written, "He gave them bread from heaven to eat."' Then Jesus said to them, 'Very truly, I tell you, it was not Moses who gave you the bread from heaven, but it is my Father who gives you the true bread from heaven. For the bread of God is that which comes down from heaven and gives life to the world.' They said to him, 'Sir, give us this bread always.' Jesus said to them, 'I am the bread of life. Whoever comes to me will never be hungry, and whoever believes in me will never be thirsty.'

The great thing about manna is that it doesn't keep—you have to eat it within hours, otherwise it goes off. No chance of building up stores of it 'for a rainy day', then. Maybe that was part of what God was teaching the desert wanderers when he sent manna from heaven to keep them going through the hard times. The word 'provision' is full of this double meaning. Provisions are what provide for our needs, but they are also provisional—they are given for the time of need, not for eternity; they are not for hoarding.

God continues to provide for our needs, day by day, even though for many of us need has turned to greed. If you have ever had to carry out a house clearance or even tidied out your own cupboards,

you will probably have come up against the human tendency to hoard so much of God's provision, 'just in case'.

In the end, we realize that all we have hoarded is useless to us on our final journey home. All that matters then is a different kind of sustenance—the bread that gives eternal life, never goes off and never runs out.

Reflection

O God, may we recognize, beyond every daily need, our eternal longings, which you alone can satisfy.

MS

Feed each other

The day was drawing to a close, and the twelve came to him and said, 'Send the crowd away, so that they may go into the surrounding villages and countryside, to lodge and get provisions; for we are here in a deserted place.' But he said to them, 'You give them something to eat.' They said, 'We have no more than five loaves and two fish—unless we are to go and buy food for all these people.' For there were about five thousand men. And he said to his disciples, 'Make them sit down in groups of about fifty each.' They did so and made them all sit down. And taking the five loaves and the two fish, he looked up to heaven, and blessed and broke them, and gave them to the disciples to set before the crowd. And all ate and were filled. What was left over was gathered up, twelve baskets of broken pieces.

I wonder what the disciples thought when Jesus turned to them with the simple—yet seemingly impossible—instruction to 'give them something to eat'. How easy it is to direct people to the nearest shop and how hard it is to provide for them ourselves, to take responsibility for each other in the way that Jesus teaches.

A story tells how, once, a man was invited to visit both heaven and hell. First, he went to hell, where he found all the tormented souls sitting at long tables, laden with all kinds of wonderful food, yet they were starving and howling with hunger. Each soul had a spoon, but the spoons were so long that they couldn't get them into their mouths. Their frustration was their torment.

Then he went to heaven and, to his amazement, there too he found the souls of the blessed, sitting at long tables, laden with all kinds of wonderful food, but they were all well fed and contented. Each had a spoon just as long as the spoons in hell, but they were able to receive all the food they needed. They were feeding each other. Their mutual service was their blessing

Reflection

Next time we are tempted to send a fellow human being elsewhere to find what they need, may we have the grace to save them the journey and feed them ourselves.

MS

I am the way, the truth and the life

'Do not let your hearts be troubled. Believe in God, believe also in me. In my Father's house there are many dwelling-places. If it were not so, would I have told you that I go to prepare a place for you? And if I go to prepare a place for you, I will come again and will take you to myself, so that where I am, there you may be also. And you know the way to the place where I am going.' Thomas said to him, 'Lord, we do not know where you are going. How can we know the way?' Jesus said to him, 'I am the way, and the truth, and the life. No one comes to the Father except through me. If you know me, you will know my Father also. From now on you do know him and have seen him.'

Planning a journey can be thrilling, but also full of trepidation. The journey of which Jesus speaks today is a journey to eternity—not just for himself, but for us all. For his friends, however, the thought of impending separation is agonizing.

When we plan a journey, we often begin with a map that shows us the route. If we are going on holiday, we may have watched TV programmes extolling the delights of the place we are going to. We may have brochures with full-colour illustrations of our destination.

Jesus doesn't offer us a map, let alone a brochure. Instead, he offers to become the way itself, as well as our constant companion as we walk along the way. He doesn't give us second-hand reports on the Kingdom, but embodies the truth about it so that we can see and experience in him and through

him the very nature of eternity with God. We don't need a glossy brochure because he gives us the richness of his lived experience and invites us to enter right into that experience.

When we arrive, he tells us, we will find that every human heart is totally at home there, each finding its own perfect place, for there are as many facets of the Kingdom as there are souls who seek it.

Prayer

O God, may we walk your way, seek your truth and live your life until we see you face to face.

MS

Walk with me

The next day John again was standing with two of his disciples, and as he watched Jesus walk by, he exclaimed, 'Look, here is the Lamb of God!' The two disciples heard him say this, and they followed Jesus. When Jesus turned and saw them following, he said to them, 'What are you looking for?' They said to him, 'Rabbi' (which translated means Teacher), 'where are you staying?' He said to them, 'Come and see.' They came and saw where he was staying, and they remained with him that day. It was about four o'clock in the afternoon. One of the two who heard John speak and followed him was Andrew, Simon Peter's brother. He first found his brother Simon and said to him, 'We have found the Messiah' (which is translated Anointed).

Even though we have the living way, how tempting it can be just to settle for a static map of our soul's journey. Even though we have the truth, how much less demanding it is to settle for second-hand reports of the Messiah. Even though we know Jesus to be the life, how much safer it is just to nod when we are told about it rather than live it! Sadly, our Christian journey can all too easily lapse into this kind of second-hand believing.

In today's passage, we hear how Jesus is inviting us into something very different. Imagine catching sight of the living Lord and somehow knowing who he is, as these two disciples did in this, their first encounter with him. Imagine all the curiosity, the desire to know all about him—where he is staying, what he is about, what makes him tick.

The questions came tumbling out, but Jesus wasn't about to answer them, at least not in the way they are expecting. Instead, he issues an invitation: 'Come and see'. He is saying, 'See for yourselves, experience me personally, then you will find the way, know the truth and live the life I offer.'

In his excitement at this first direct encounter, Andrew runs off to tell his brother about Jesus, but Simon Peter will, in his turn, also have to walk the way himself into a personal encounter with Jesus. Second-hand will never be good enough.

Reflection

As we walk the way and learn to trust the truth, may our second-hand believing turn into a first-hand living faith.

MS

I am the true vine

'I am the true vine, and my Father is the vinegrower. He removes every branch in me that bears no fruit. Every branch that bears fruit he prunes to make it bear more fruit… Abide in me as I abide in you. Just as the branch cannot bear fruit by itself unless it abides in the vine, neither can you unless you abide in me. I am the vine and you are the branches. Those who abide in me and I in them bear much fruit, because apart from me you can do nothing. Whoever does not abide in me is thrown away like a branch and withers… If you abide in me, and my words abide in you, ask for whatever you wish and it will be done for you. My Father is glorified by this, that you bear much fruit and become my disciples.'

When I was a child, we lived very close to a wood and, in May, it became especially magical, with its vibrant carpet of bluebells. The sight and scent of bluebells growing wild in the woods has always remained for me a symbol of a very happy childhood.

When my daughter was born, I came home with her from hospital to a garden full of golden daffodils, which had come into bloom during the three days I had been away. The sight and scent of fresh daffodils remains a symbol for me of all the joy that comes with motherhood.

However, I could never resist the temptation as a child to gather armfuls of the beautiful bluebells to take home and put in a vase. The living flowers I plucked at dawn were drooping by noon and dead by dusk. I learned my lesson quickly—that if I cut them away from their roots, they could not survive.

By the time my daughter was born I had learned not to make the same mistake with the daffodils. Though they last longer than bluebells, like all flowers, daffodils die when plucked. Slowly I am learning from the flowers something deeply important about myself.

Reflection and prayer

A vase of cut flowers may last for a week, but the living plant will last a lifetime. O God, cut off from you, we cannot survive a day; rooted in you, we will live forever.

MS

89

Abide in me

'As the Father has loved me, so I have loved you; abide in my love. If you keep my commandments, you will abide in my love, just as I have kept my Father's commandments and abide in his love. I have said these things to you so that my joy may be in you, and that your joy may be complete. This is my commandment, that you love one another as I have loved you. No one has greater love than this, to lay down one's life for one's friends. You are my friends if you do what I command you. I do not call you servants any longer, because the servant does not know what the master is doing; but I have called you friends, because I have made known to you everything that I have heard from my Father. You did not choose me but I chose you. And I appointed you to go and bear fruit, fruit that will last.'

The English word 'abide' has its roots in the Anglo-Saxon word 'abidan', which carried several layers of meaning.

The first of these is 'to dwell or reside'. How can we dwell in God's love? One way is to seek to enter into his presence deliberately on a regular basis in prayer. Another way is to heighten our awareness of God's constant presence in everything and everyone around us by reflecting each day on where and how we have encountered God in particular ways.

A second layer of meaning in the Anglo-Saxon is 'to wait'. We have retained this meaning in the phrase 'to bide our time'. To abide in God, then, is also about waiting. We measure our time in minutes and days, but time is merely a human device. We will only experience the fullness of God's dream if we are willing to wait and watch as it unfolds silently through the eons.

A third layer of meaning is 'to remain alive'. We will remain alive if we stay rooted and grounded in the source of our being, never allowing any lesser concerns to sever that connection, and shed our illusion that we can 'go it alone'.

Reflection

O God, may we know you in our daily living, trust you in the waiting and live in you through every moment of each day.

MS

I am the resurrection and the life

When Jesus arrived, he found that Lazarus had already been in the tomb for four days. Now Bethany was near Jerusalem, some two miles away, and many of the Jews had come to Martha and Mary to console them about their brother. When Martha heard that Jesus was coming, she went and met him, while Mary stayed at home. Martha said to Jesus, 'Lord, if you had been here, my brother would not have died. But even now I know that God will give you whatever you ask of him.' Jesus said to her, 'Your brother will rise again.' Martha said to him, 'I know that he will rise again in the resurrection on the last day.' Jesus said to her, 'I am the resurrection and the life. Those who believe in me, even though they die, will live, and everyone who lives and believes in me will never die. Do you believe this?'

In today's reading a long, dark shadow lies over the little home in Bethany where Jesus had so often enjoyed the friendship and hospitality of his close friends, Martha, Mary and Lazarus. Now those happy memories are cloaked in grief. Not just straightforward grief, either, but grief with an edge of anger and bewilderment, hence the reproach, 'If you had been here, my brother would not have died.'

We, of course, know that Lazarus will live again, but for those directly affected at the time, the shadow was dark indeed. They could not have known that something new was already happening in the depths of that shadow.

Perhaps you too recall times when your life has been overshadowed by a situation, an anxiety, a memory or destructive relationship. Perhaps that shadow has darkened your life for many years. If so, may today's 'I am' declaration be an encouragement to you. Something good is growing and forming in the darkness. Life almost always begins in darkness—the darkness of the womb, the earth, the tomb. When Jesus describes himself as the resurrection and the life, he is asserting a stupendous fact—that life is the permanent reality beneath every cloak of death, not just in some distant heaven, but here and now and always.

Reflection

The darkness that we fear is, in fact, the cradle for the new life that we long for.

MS

MATTHEW 28:16–20 (NRSV)

I am with you always

Now the eleven disciples went to Galilee, to the mountain to which Jesus had directed them. When they saw him, they worshipped him; but some doubted. And Jesus came and said to them, 'All authority in heaven and on earth has been given to me. Go therefore and make disciples of all nations, baptizing them in the name of the Father and of the Son and of the Holy Spirit, and teaching them to obey everything that I have commanded you. And remember, I am with you always, to the end of the age.'

For years I felt that somehow I had to conjure up God's presence (or at least a felt sense of that presence) when I prayed. It seemed as if it was all down to me and my own efforts. Needless to say, those efforts usually came to naught.

Then I came across a story by the Jesuit priest Anthony de Mello. He tells how once a little fish was swimming in the vast ocean. He had heard a rumour about this thing called 'ocean' and he wanted very much to find it and feel it and see it. In his quest to discover the ocean, this little fish asked many other fish in the sea, 'Have you heard about "ocean"? Do you know where I might find it?' The answer always came back, 'No. We have heard the rumour, too, but we have never seen "ocean" and we don't know where it might be.'

Who knows how the story ended? Perhaps the fish gave up the search and dismissed 'ocean' as a figment of his imagination.

What about us? We live and move and have our being in the ocean of God's love. There is no need to search. Without that ocean we have no being. Our lives are swimming in God.

So it is that we end our weeks with Jesus' 'I am' sayings with an 'I am' that, technically, is not one of the seven, yet is so fundamental to our journey we need to keep on hearing it. There is no need to search, no need for fear, no way that we can be separated from the ocean of Jesus' continuing and ever-present love.

Reflection

We are because God is—now and eternally.

MS

1 KINGS 19:19–21 (NRSV)

Barbecue of decision

So he [Elijah] set out from there, and found Elisha son of Shaphat, who was ploughing. There were twelve yoke of oxen ahead of him, and he was with the twelfth. Elijah passed by him and threw his mantle over him. He left the oxen, ran after Elijah, and said, 'Let me kiss my father and my mother, and then I will follow you.' Then Elijah said to him, 'Go back again; for what have I done to you?' He returned from following him, took the yoke of oxen, and slaughtered them; using the equipment from the oxen, he boiled their flesh, and gave it to the people, and they ate. Then he set out and followed Elijah, and became his servant.

There was no quiet enquiry such as, 'Would you like to consider a career change?' Subtlety was never Elijah's style. This was a challenge, direct and demanding. God had picked Elisha out (v. 16). Now Elijah was calling him into service and there was no thought at all of Elisha saying 'No'.

Suddenly Elijah's cloak rested on Elisha's shoulders. This was the cloak Elijah had wrapped around his face when he stood at the mouth of the cave and listened to the voice of God (v. 13). Was there still a smell in its folds of dust and smoke from the earthquake, wind and fire? Responsibility, duty and burden were part of the fabric.

What do you look for when you start to trust God's work to a successor? Commitment is essential. Elisha's ox roast, fuelled by the wood of his plough, left him without a safety net. There would be no

easy going back. Character is important, too. Sharing the feast with family and friends let them know what Elisha was about. He was not afraid to be seen in a new role, but he was still his parents' son. He said farewell properly.

'What have I done to you?' said Elijah. Perhaps the words meant, 'This is your moment of calling. You work out how to follow it. Be committed, but be yourself, too.' The barbecue was Elisha's way of accepting a new calling and thanking the people who had shaped his life so far.

Reflection and prayer

Thank God for the people whose love has shaped your life. Ask God for courage to be ready when new calling comes.

JP

Pilgrim prophet

Now when the Lord was about to take Elijah up to heaven by a whirlwind, Elijah and Elisha were on their way from Gilgal. Elijah said to Elisha, 'Stay here; for the Lord has sent me as far as Bethel.' But Elisha said, 'As the Lord lives, and as you yourself live, I will not leave you.' So they went down to Bethel. The company of prophets who were in Bethel came out to Elisha and said to him, 'Do you know that today the Lord will take your master away from you?' And he said, 'Yes, I know; keep silent.'

Many places in the Bible show a handover of grace, from one generation to another. In every era God seeks out believing men and women to carry forward the work of those who went before, but sometimes you see it sharply focused in one particular incident. Elijah handing over to Elisha is that sort of occasion.

The chapter begins with a mood of wonder. Elijah will be taken up. You sense that Elisha understands what an awesome moment this was going be. Yet, this is a meandering journey—in the travelling and in the telling. Three times Elijah said 'stay' and three times Elisha refuses (vv. 2, 4, 6). Their fellow prophets are a kind of chorus line (vv. 3, 5, 7). They know what is happening to the main actors, but they cannot really get involved.

This experience would prove Elisha's loyalty to and care of Elijah. It would also teach him

something fresh about God. The journey was to be a pilgrimage, the way to a holy place.

Elijah and Elisha have a message that speaks to the transitions in our own lives. We find God's way into the future by honouring the past and bringing it to the best conclusion we can. Even in the most difficult transition of all—when someone is near to death—it is often right to sit with them for as long as possible. To wait until waiting is done, to follow as far as we can just now, is a wholesome and holy thing, not just for them but for us, too. It allows for a proper ending and helps us to take the first slow steps of a new beginning.

Prayer

God of eternity, help us not to fear times of change and transition, but meet them as moments of grace and of promise.

JP

Coated with responsibility

Elijah said to Elisha, 'Tell me what I may do for you before I am taken from you.' Elisha said, 'Please let me inherit a double share of your spirit.' He responded, 'You have asked a hard thing; yet, if you see me as I am being taken from you, it will be granted you; if not, it will not.' As they continued walking and talking, a chariot of fire and horses of fire separated the two of them, and Elijah ascended in a whirlwind into heaven. Elisha kept watching and crying out, 'Father, father! The chariots of Israel and its horsemen!' But when he could no longer see him, he grasped his own clothes and tore them in two pieces.

Elisha asked for a double share of Elijah's spirit. While a host of people had been helped by the general influence of Elijah's ministry, Elisha needed a more personal blessing. He wanted the eldest son's share of the legacy, to equip him to lead the family of Israel spiritually and bear the burdens and expectations of others. 'That depends,' said Elijah, 'on your seeing me depart.'

Elijah knew that he could not simply hand on his spirit to Elisha. Spiritual experience can never be passed on intact from one person to another. Elisha needed his own vision of God and the moment of Elijah's departure was the time to find it. Heaven would be open and the Spirit of God could touch Elisha in ways that marked him profoundly.

When the moment came, Elisha saw a great army around them. He realized the strength and presence of God. He was not alone, nor was the nation he would serve. The chariots and horsemen of Israel became a theme of his ministry (6:15–17; 7:6; 13:14). This was an experience to shape his life and to share in times of crisis.

Elisha tore his clothes as a release for his grief and distress. His master, mentor, father, was gone, but he could discard these torn garments. From then on he would carry the mantle of Elijah and all it represented. With the vision came responsibility. Elisha takes up the mantle and makes his way back towards the people.

Prayer
Lord, when you call me to new service, please give me a fresh vision of your strength and presence.

JP

Running on empty

Now the wife of a member of the company of the prophets cried to Elisha, 'Your servant my husband is dead; and you know that your servant feared the Lord, but a creditor has come to take my two children as slaves... Your servant has nothing in the house except a jar of oil.' He said, 'Go outside, borrow vessels from all your neighbours... and start pouring into all these vessels; when each is full set it aside... Go sell the oil and pay your debts, and you and your children can live on the rest.'

Elisha is remembered as a miracle man, bringing the renewing power of God into a host of situations. Sometimes he was drawn into public affairs, to avert a national danger. More often his miracles were private—deeds of compassion for needy people. Elisha knew the people and moved among them. In many ways, his ministry foreshadows that of Jesus. A number of the incidents described are very similar to episodes in the Gospels.

The prophet's widow was in a desperate plight. Grief and loss were hard enough to bear, but her bereavement had brought poverty, too, and, if she could not repay what she owed, her children would be taken as slaves. Yet Elisha brought hope out of despair, made much of the little that she had and left her able to clear the debt and support her family. His actions brought them out of the shadow of slavery so they could be free. The

redeemer God of the exodus was alive and at work.

This tragedy came to a godly family (v. 1). Faith does not always keep hardship at bay, but it gives us an extra resource with which to meet it. With faith goes fellowship—we can do things for each other. When sorrow visits a home, the Elisha tradition—and the Jesus tradition, too—is to reach out with compassion and give practical help. Grief may be doubly difficult if it leads on to forced and unwelcome change. The involvement of caring friends can make a difference, open new options and choices and help to make the future possible.

Reflection and prayer

In some places in the world, debt still leads to slavery. Pray for the people affected. Can you find out what is being done to challenge this practice?

JP

Home improvement

One day Elisha was passing through Shunem, where a wealthy woman lived, who urged him to have a meal. So whenever he passed that way, he would stop there for a meal. She said to her husband, 'Look, I am sure that this man who regularly passes our way is a holy man of God. Let us make a small roof chamber with walls, and put there for him a bed, a table, a chair, and a lamp, so that he can stay there whenever he comes to us.'

Elisha was a strong character. He did not lean constantly on other people, but here he is glad to accept help that is offered sincerely and cheerfully. As he travelled about, this place was to be a refuge, a sanctuary in which to rest, hide and pray. Here he could draw breath, connect with God and get ready for new work. Everyone needs such a space and sometimes it is busy people who need it most.

This modest house extension has been called a little temple, a small-scale shrine. In this period of history, the Hebrew people were a divided nation. The southern kingdom of Judah had Jerusalem as its capital and the Lord's temple was there, but the northern territory of Israel, centred on the town of Samaria, was always tempted to follow other loyalties and lords. Elisha was a prophet of Israel and Shunem was deep in the northern countryside.

So, for some of the community in the north, Elisha represented the Lord's presence, as surely as the temple and its worship did in the south. His ministry brought the love of God to life among the people. Elisha's local retreat house surely became a source of renewing grace and power for him and, through him, for others. It reminds us of another upper room, where the Church met with God (Mark 14:15; Acts 1:13) and went out in the power of the Spirit. God worked through Elisha, too. In time, he gave new life and healing to this family in Shunem who had welcomed him so warmly (2 Kings 4:11–37). The memory of what he had done lingered and lasted, as we shall see (8:1–6).

Reflection

Many people today live at a distance from the Church and its life. For some, you may be their main point of contact with God.

JP

General medicine

Naaman, commander of the army of the king of Aram, was a great man and in high favour with his master, because by him the Lord had given victory to Aram. The man, though a mighty warrior, suffered from leprosy. Now the Arameans on one of their raids had taken a young girl captive from the land of Israel, and she served Naaman's wife. She said to her mistress, 'If only my lord were with the prophet who is in Samaria! He would cure him of his leprosy.' So Naaman went in and told his lord just what the girl from the land of Israel had said. And the king of Aram said, 'Go then, and I will send along a letter to the king of Israel.'

The story about Naaman is a bridge between two sides of Elisha's ministry—the public and political on one hand and the personal and pastoral on the other. Naaman was a Syrian soldier and a major public figure in his own land, but now he was desperate. This skin disease (even if it was not what we would call leprosy today) could cut a man off from his community and career, making him an outcast.

The young servant girl is one of the heroines of the Bible. She lived in a difficult situation—an exile, a slave, separated from her home and hopes and loves. Nonetheless, she spoke from faith and intervened to save Naaman from falling into an exile of his own. She still believes in God's power even though circumstances have taken her away from the places and people who nurtured her faith.

So, Naaman rides off with a letter to the king of Israel. Is this royal good manners—going through the proper channels? It seems not (v. 6). It is short-sightedness, from a king who thinks that all power resides in royal palaces, even the power to heal. Of course it doesn't and Naaman will learn to think in new ways before he gets back home. Perhaps he was already starting to do this, when he listened to a slave girl and let himself be led by her faith.

Prayer

God of the unexpected, help me to listen for your voice in humble people. Help me, too, to be ready to speak a word for you among those who face fear and need.

JP

Adult learning

[Elisha] sent a message to the king, '… Let him come to me, that he may learn that there is a prophet in Israel.' So Naaman came with his horses and chariots, and halted at the entrance of Elisha's house. Elisha sent a messenger to him, saying, 'Go, wash in the Jordan seven times, and your flesh shall be restored and you shall be clean.' But Naaman became angry and went away… '… Are not Abana and Pharpar, the rivers of Damascus, better than all the waters of Israel? Could I not wash in them, and be clean?'

After Naaman's awkward visit to the king of Israel (vv. 6–7), Elisha stepped in to rescue the situation: 'Let him come to me', but, even so, this was not a happy meeting for either man. Elisha was not at all impressed by the string of chariots parked in the street and, if Naaman expected a formal welcome, as befitted an important fellow like himself, he was disappointed. There was no red carpet, no prophet, no obvious prayers, no ritual or dignity or sign. There was just a servant, with a message: 'Go to the Jordan and wash.'

Naaman went off in a huff. He wanted personal attention. If all Israel could offer was a river, then he had a couple of those at home. Why should he demean himself and wash in the Jordan, on the orders of a prophet who had not bothered to meet him?

Eventually, Naaman's staff talked him down from his high horse. He would have done some-thing difficult, if the prophet had told him to (v. 13), so why not do this, which is much more straight-forward? So off went the chariots to wait by the Jordan while Naaman dived in. He discovered that he was clean and whole again (v. 14).

'Salvation is from the Jews' (John 4:22). The maker of heaven and earth is Israel's ancient Lord. Naaman had to learn this and dis-cover God in a way that he had never done before. He found him-self too. He came out of the river and was not just clean on the out-side, but humbled on the inside. God is not much impressed by our earthly rank or riches, but he is still for us, which matters more than everything.

Prayer

Lord, make me humble enough to receive all that you want to give me.

JP

Thanks and no thanks

Then he [Naaman] returned to the man of God, he and all his company; he came and stood before him and said, 'Now I know that there is no God in all the earth except in Israel; please accept a present from your servant.' But he said, 'As the Lord lives, whom I serve, I will accept nothing!'… But when Naaman had gone from him a short distance, Gehazi, the servant of Elisha the man of God, thought, 'My master has let that Aramean Naaman off too lightly… I will run after him and get something out of him.'

Naaman, with commendable honesty and humility, came back to say thanks. Once again the chariots rolled up Elisha's street. This time the prophet came out to meet the general and Naaman offered him wealth and plenty. He was not trying to buy God's favour, but just wanted to say a proper 'Thank you'.

Elisha declined the offer. He did not need the gifts and would not take credit for the healing. Naaman had started his journey with the promise that the prophet would cure him physically (v. 3), but, once he is healed, he starts to talk about God (v. 15). Elisha wanted Naaman to remember the Lord. Refusing the gifts would remind him of where the glory belonged.

Gehazi is a tragic figure. He helped Elisha for a while, but his master's faith and character never quite rubbed off on him. Working for the prophet had given him a position in life, to exploit for his own ends. Possibly Gehazi did not start like this and perhaps this was an isolated mistake, but it was a terribly bad one. He made a holy moment an occasion for deceit and profit.

When Gehazi got back home, Elisha knew what had happened. Prophets are like that. The chapter ends with Naaman's leprosy attaching itself to Gehazi (v. 27). Gehazi is a warning to us to watch our honesty and deal straightforwardly with everyone. The reasoning that goes something like, 'I deserve it. They can afford it. There's no harm in it' seems very plausible at times—it did to Gehazi—but it can be a very unreliable moral compass.

Prayer

Lord, when I keep company with good and faithful people, help me to learn from the best in their lives and grow in wisdom and truth.

JP

Losing the edge

Now the company of prophets said to Elisha… 'Let us go to the Jordan, and let us collect logs there, one for each of us, and build a place there for us to live.'… But as one was felling a log, his axe-head fell into the water; he cried out, 'Alas, master! It was borrowed.' Then the man of God said, 'Where did it fall?' When they showed him the place, he cut off a stick and threw it in there, and made the iron float. He said, 'Pick it up.' So he reached out his hand and took it.

When the rollercoaster in the English seaside resort of Blackpool was rebuilt in 2007, they drained the lake beneath. In the mud was a valuable earring, which had been lost by a celebrity who visited the town in 1934 and rode on the rollercoaster. She was, it is said, very attached to the earring, but it was obviously not well attached to her. Water can swallow up our property if we are not careful and sometimes we never get it back.

An axe-head was a piece of high-tech equipment in the Iron Age. To get a rough sense of its worth, think of something like a computer or a car in our day. Losing a borrowed axe was serious. In a land where people lived close to the breadline, many would not have been able to pay for it.

An ancient Christian reading of this passage links the wood Elisha threw into the river to the death of Jesus, as the cross is the wood that restores our losses. There we are put right with God and given the chance to start again. There, peace is made and lives made whole. God can restore opportunities and hopes we thought were gone for ever.

The phrase 'company of the prophets' appears on several occasions in these chapters. They are disciples of a sort, nurturing their own spiritual lives under Elisha's guidance. As Elisha does here, a leader must sometimes solve other people's problems, but the best spiritual leaders also help their followers to look directly to God and discover the depths of love and power in the cross of Christ.

Prayer

Pray for someone you know who is coping with loss—of a job, home, family member, health. Ask God to give them hope.

JP

2 Kings 6:15–20 (NRSV, abridged)

Open and shut

An army with horses and chariots was all around the city. His [Elisha's] servant said, 'Alas, master! What shall we do?' He replied, 'Do not be afraid, for there are more with us than there are with them.' Then Elisha prayed: 'O Lord, please open his eyes that he may see.' So the Lord opened the eyes of the servant, and he saw; the mountain was full of horses and chariots of fire all around Elisha. When the Arameans came down against him, Elisha prayed to the Lord, and said, 'Strike this people, please, with blindness.' … And he led them to Samaria. As soon as they entered Samaria, Elisha said, 'O Lord, open the eyes of these men so that they may see.'

We have come to the political side of Elisha's ministry. His prophetic insight was a major weapon for Israel in fending off the Syrian army, so the Syrians came to capture him. His servant is anxious, but Elisha seems to keep his cool. His attitude is that it's all a matter of vision. Three times he prays about this—for sight, blindness and then sight again.

First he asks for his servant to be able to see. This is the same vision Elisha had when Elijah was taken (2:11–12). The hosts of God are keeping watch and they outnumber any human army. Even amid the turbulence and stresses of time, the earth is thick with grace. God knows what goes on and when we pray he gets involved.

Then Elisha prays for the enemy forces to be blinded and asks innocently, 'Can I help you?' like an old-time Boy Scout showing someone across the street (6:19). Only when the men are impounded in Samaria do their eyes open, when it is too late for battle or even negotiation.

The episode ends with Elisha as peacemaker. He points out that the Syrians have not been captured in battle and the king of Israel has no right to kill them. So, they are given a decent meal, sent back to their commander and they stopped raiding Israel (vv. 21–23). As so often in the Old Testament, this is a touch of the gospel. Sometimes loving our enemies (Matthew 5:44) can help to defuse the ill feeling that divides us.

Prayer

God of invisible power, help me to see your purpose and presence, even when I am alarmed and anxious.

JP

2 KINGS 6:24–31 (NRSV, ABRIDGED)

Desperate days

King Ben-hadad of Aram mustered his entire army; he marched against Samaria and laid siege to it. As the siege continued... as the king of Israel was walking on the city wall, a woman cried out to him... 'This woman said to me, "Give up your son; we will eat him today, and we will eat my son tomorrow." So we cooked my son and ate him... But she has hidden her son.' When the king heard the words of the woman... he said, 'So may God do to me, and more, if the head of Elisha son of Shaphat stays on his shoulders today.'

Only people who have lived through a long siege—and there are still many who have—will really understand the stresses behind this passage. When a community is shut in, fearful, starving and desperate, then dignity and decency will struggle to stay alive. Cruelty and concealment seem necessary survival strategies and even good neighbours find trust harder than it used to be.

This Syrian invasion was on a larger scale than before. It may have been a response to a period of famine (8:1), to secure food for Syria at Israel's expense. If so, then the people in Samaria were doubly afflicted, with the siege coming after a long spell of scarcity and rising prices. The dreadful deal struck by the two women shows how extreme the situation had become.

In times of trouble, people look to their leaders and suddenly the burden was too great for the king to bear. The horror that had come to his people made him lash out: 'Bring me the head of Elisha. Kill the man whose ideas and loyalties are never as straightforward as they should be. Blame God.'

That is not good kingship. Leaders are usually best dealing with their stresses away from the public eye, but, when someone hits out at heaven, God may be less alarmed than we are. There is strong and angry language in the Bible. Some of the Psalms offer a pattern of prayer that is honest rather than tidy. In the cross of Jesus, God comes face to face with sin and anger, bears it and turns evil into good.

Reflection and prayer

Remember places where hunger and fear stalk the streets and pray for the people who lead and speak for God there.

JP

Day of good news

Now there were four leprous men outside the city gate, who said to one another, 'Why should we sit here until we die?... So they arose at twilight to go to the Aramean camp; but when they came to the edge of the Aramean camp, there was no one there... they went into a tent, ate and drank, carried off silver, gold, and clothing, and went and hid them... Then they said to one another, 'What we are doing is wrong. This is a day of good news; if we are silent and wait until the morning light, we will be found guilty; therefore let us go and tell the king's household.'

In siege conditions, these four men would have been at the back of the food queue. No one bothered much about lepers when there was little to share. In the end, they decided that there was nothing to lose in going to the enemy. Food was there and perhaps their lives would be spared. So they were the first to discover that the whole camp was empty. It was almost like Easter morning. As with Syria, so with death—God had driven the enemy away.

The odd thing is the way people reacted. The four men forgot that others would want to know. They were caught up in their own good fortune, not thinking of anyone else. Then, when they did share the news, the king would not believe it. He thought it was a trick (v. 12), but the Aramean army had indeed run for home. The 'chariots and horsemen of Israel' had frightened them away (v. 6; as in 2:12; 6:17).

Elisha had said there would be plenty of food (7:1). Sometimes no one believes a prophet—that is, until his words come true (v. 2) and, even when they do, the world struggles to handle the good news. The same sometimes happens with the gospel. People then and now wonder if it can really be true—good out of evil, hope out of despair, resurrection out of the tomb of God. We must remember that every day is a day of good news—it was true yesterday, is today and will be tomorrow. If we hesitate to share it, people's spirits will grow thin and love, joy and peace will be casualties of the famine.

Prayer

God of hope and risen life, give your Church courage and joy in sharing your word and your love, for Jesus' sake.

JP

No man's land

Now the king was talking with Gehazi the servant of the man of God, saying, 'Tell me all the great things that Elisha has done.' While he was telling the king how Elisha had restored a dead person to life, the woman whose son he had restored to life appealed to the king for her house and her land. Gehazi said, 'My lord king, here is the woman, and here is her son whom Elisha restored to life.' When the king questioned the woman, she told him. So the king appointed an official for her, saying, 'Restore all that was hers, together with all the revenue of the fields from the day that she left the land until now.'

Elisha does not even appear in this reading, but his reputation is enough to influence events. The woman of Shunem, from chapter 4, had left home as famine loomed and was gone seven years. In the meantime, someone else acquired her land. Now she wants to recover it and comes to seek justice from the king (vv. 1–3).

Women in that society did not usually speak in court, but her husband was older (4:14) and may even have died by this time. She was vulnerable, as widows often are, but, as she arrived, there was a happy coincidence. The king had asked about Elisha and Gehazi had just told him about the raising of the woman's son (4:18–37), when in she came.

No doubt the king's sympathy was aroused and he may have thought, 'If God has blessed this family, perhaps I'd better do the same'. Some suggest another reason for the king's actions. Gehazi's testimony to 'the great things Elisha did' opened the king's mind to a more godly way of looking at life. Issues of justice, need, poverty and grievance became more important to him. He started using his power in a different way.

We cannot tell whether the king's behaviour lasted or this was an isolated judgment, but there is surely a pattern to discern in this story. Hearing about the great acts of God should always open our minds and hearts to needy neighbours. The gospel invites us to live more fairly and truly. Listening to the word and acting on it belong together (James 1:22).

Reflection and prayer

Remember anyone you know of who is vulnerable and needs to be treated fairly. Pray for them.

JP

Old enemies

Now when Elisha had fallen sick with the illness of which he was to die, King Joash of Israel went down to him, and wept before him, crying, 'My father, my father! The chariots of Israel and its horsemen!' Elisha said to him, 'Take a bow and arrows... Open the window to the east... Shoot'; and he shot. Then he said, 'The Lord's arrow of victory, the arrow of victory over Aram!'... He continued, 'Take the arrows'; and he took them. He said to the king of Israel, 'Strike the ground with them'; he struck three times, and stopped. Then the man of God was angry with him.

Elisha ministered under five of Israel's kings and, as he lay dying, the fifth of these, Joash, sought him out. The king's words—'The chariots of Israel and its horsemen!'—match exactly what Elisha said when Elijah was taken (2:12). Elisha had lived close to God and his faith had been a mighty presence for Israel's armies, like a contingent of the very hosts of heaven.

Defence mattered in these fragile times. The Arameans, from Syria, were a persistent thorn in Israel's side. So, when Elisha ordered Joash to shoot the arrow, he meant this as an acted parable, a symbol of faith and battle. The arrow stood for the Lord's power, aimed at the east, towards Aram. Victory comes from the Lord, was Elisha's point. Prophets come and go, but you can still trust God.

Yet, Joash lacked some vital spark of faith. Elisha urged him, 'Strike. Act out your battles. Use the arrows with energy and force. Trust God's power.' Then Joash stopped. Perhaps he lacked conviction. Certainly, according to this chapter (v. 11), he lacked any deep relationship with the Lord. Elisha saw that his word had fallen into shallow soil. An old failing—royal lack of faith—would lead to indecisive wars and hollow victories. Aram would continue to batter on the door.

Here we see some old enemies. Aram was one and the king's spiritual weakness was another. There was a third enemy, too, which Elisha faced—death, the last foe we meet on the journey of faith. That enemy has since been destroyed forever by the cross and risen life of Jesus.

Prayer

My foes are ever near me,
around me and within.
But Jesus, draw thou nearer...'

John E. Bode (1816–74)

JP

Jesus' family

If you were asked to name Jesus' family, whom would you list? Obviously Mary and Joseph; perhaps Anna and Joachim—traditionally the names of Mary's parents; perhaps his 'brothers and sisters' who appear fleetingly in some of the Gospels.

Going further back, you might know some of the names from the genealogy with which Matthew begins his Gospel and certainly that Jesus was 'of the house of David'.

If you've read some recent bestselling books, you might wonder if Mary Magdalene should be counted in and even whether or not there were children of a secret marriage, through whom the blood of Jesus has come down through the generations—a royal bloodline. I wonder if the popularity of some of these claims (for which there seems no evidence in the Gospels whatsoever) comes from a belief that only a blood relationship could connect us to Jesus?

Jesus' own teachings on family are quite ambivalent. He certainly supports the idea of the permanence of marriage and values children in a way that is quite at odds with the prevailing culture of his time. However, on the other hand, he speaks of the necessity for his disciples to be willing to leave everything and follow him—parents, husbands, wives, children, property. He challenges his disciples to put the gospel first, against all the expectations of his society, in order to gain eternal life.

It can sound as though Jesus is decrying intimate relationships and proposing that we live a very isolated and lonely life, but the reality is quite different. He obviously valued friendship and homes where he could relax, such as that of Mary, Martha and Lazarus at Bethany. He also broadens the concept of family beyond the confines of blood relationship, speaking of his disciples as his brothers and sisters and mothers, drawing them into his own relationship with the Father, so that they can all become children of God. Paul builds on the idea, speaking of Christians being the adopted children of God, able to address him as Abba and share in Jesus' victory over death.

Jesus' family is one of faith, not of blood, and everyone can belong. As his disciples, we can all be his brothers, sisters, mothers, and he is a brother to each of us.

Helen Julian CSF

Who do you think you are?

An account of the genealogy of Jesus the Messiah, the son of David, the son of Abraham. Abraham was the father of Isaac, and Isaac the father of Jacob, and Jacob the father of Judah and his brothers... and Salmon the father of Boaz by Rahab, and Boaz the father of Obed by Ruth, and Obed the father of Jesse, and Jesse the father of King David. And David was the father of Solomon by the wife of Uriah... So all the generations from Abraham to David are fourteen generations; and from David to the deportation to Babylon, fourteen generations; and from the deportation to Babylon to the Messiah, fourteen generations.

The genealogies in the Bible can seem rather irrelevant. We're tempted to skip over them and get on to the rest of the story of salvation. In fact, these lists are crucial to the story—not just to the biblical story but also to our own stories.

There is a fascination with genealogy today that bears witness to the importance of roots, to knowing where we've come from. The popularity of books and TV programmes on the subject such as *Who Do You Think You Are?* witness to a fascination with other people's stories as well as our own.

So, what can this list (perhaps you may now be tempted to go and read the entire list) tell us about Jesus? At the very beginning, it places him in his context—in the line of David, God's anointed king, and Abraham, the first to make a covenant with God. Many of the other names are also great ones in

the Bible—Isaac, Jacob, Solomon.

Then come the unexpected names—the women's names. The genealogy is traced through the male line, but just occasionally the mother is also included. When we study these names, they are unexpected and irregular, somehow at odds with the other names in the list. They are, if you like, the skeletons in the cupboard of Jesus' genealogy.

Researchers say that every family tree has such skeletons and I suspect that sometimes they're the most interesting of our ancestors, the ones we come to appreciate the most. Tomorrow we'll see what these unexpected women tell us about Jesus.

Reflection

From whom are you proud to be descended?

HJ CSF

Son of David, Son of God

Now the birth of Jesus the Messiah took place in this way. When his mother Mary had been engaged to Joseph, but before they lived together, she was found to be with child from the Holy Spirit. Her husband Joseph... planned to dismiss her quietly. But just when he had resolved to do this, an angel of the Lord appeared to him in a dream and said, 'Joseph, son of David, do not be afraid to take Mary as your wife, for the child conceived in her is from the Holy Spirit. She will bear a son, and you are to name him Jesus, for he will save his people from their sins.'

Mary is the last of five women mentioned in Matthew's genealogy of Jesus. All are in some way irregular, not always respectable.

Tamar (1:3) conceived her twins, Perez and Zerah, by her father-in-law, Judah (Genesis 38:6). Rahab was a prostitute in Jericho who helped the spies sent by Joshua and so was spared when the Israelites took the city (Joshua 2: 6). Ruth was a Moabite woman and, therefore, not one of the chosen people, yet she became David's grandmother. The wife of Uriah was, of course, Bathsheba who had an adulterous relationship with King David. He had Uriah killed so that he could have Bathsheba as his wife (2 Samuel 11).

Looked at like that, they're not paragons of virtue and Mary must have looked rather the same to those around her. Pregnant before she was married, they would have suspected the worst, as did Joseph.

As with the other women in the genealogy, however, God is at work in these irregular circumstances. Perhaps Matthew places them in his genealogy just to prepare us for the most breathtaking claim of all. Not content with tracing the line of the Messiah through prostitutes, adulterers and foreigners, now he tells of a child who has no human father because he is from the Holy Spirit. Through Joseph, he is a son of David and, through the Holy Spirit, he is the Son of God. Just as Joshua brought the Israelites into the promised land, this new Joshua (Jesus is the same name) will bring God's people, all of them—the respectable and the not—into salvation.

Prayer

Son of David, Son of God, strengthen my faith in your ability to work through the unexpected.

HJ CSF

Birthing the word

In the sixth month the angel Gabriel was sent by God to a town in Galilee called Nazareth, to a virgin engaged to a man whose name was Joseph, of the house of David. The virgin's name was Mary. And he came to her and said, 'Greetings, favoured one! The Lord is with you... And now, you will conceive in your womb and bear a son, and you will name him Jesus. He will be great, and will be called the Son of the Most High, and the Lord God will give to him the throne of his ancestor David.'

This is such a well-known passage, familiar from myriad nativity plays and carol services. Luke's telling of the story is, as so often, from the woman's point of view and very particular. We have the time and place and names of those involved. In the sixth month of Elizabeth's pregnancy (itself an unexpected act of God), Gabriel comes to Mary and brings her stunning news.

She is pregnant with the son of God, whom she is to name Jesus, which means 'God is salvation'. The people of Israel had for much of their history seen themselves collectively as in some sense God's firstborn son (Exodus 4:22; Jeremiah 31:20; Hosea 11:1). David and the line of kings who followed felt they embodied that relationship in a particular way (2 Samuel 7:14, Psalm 2:7, 89:27). At the time of this story, however, there had been 200 years of kings of Israel who were not of David's line. Herod, for example, was a military commander made king by the Romans.

Then, God comes to another unexpected woman and gives her the momentous news that she is to give birth to the true king of Israel, the son whose relationship with the Father has been the pattern for the relationship of God and his people down the centuries.

Mary hears the word of God and accepts it, allowing it to act on her. In this way she becomes worthy to bring forth the word, the word that brought creation into being and will now begin to bring to birth a new people and a new creation.

Prayer

God of creation and redemption, may I hear your word and allow it to be born in me today.

HJ CSF

Keeping it in the family

In those days Mary set out and went with haste to a Judean town in the hill country, where she entered the house of Zechariah and greeted Elizabeth. When Elizabeth heard Mary's greeting, the child leaped in her womb. And Elizabeth was filled with the Holy Spirit and exclaimed with a loud cry, 'Blessed are you among women, and blessed is the fruit of your womb. And why has this happened to me, that the mother of my Lord comes to me? For as soon as I heard the sound of your greeting, the child in my womb leaped for joy. And blessed is she who believed that there would be a fulfilment of what was spoken to her by the Lord.'

There's an old joke among Franciscans that only God knows how many Franciscans there are in the world. Francis has inspired so many people to follow Christ in his footsteps in so many different ways that no one can keep count of them all. As a Franciscan myself, I know that there's a family resemblance among us all, despite our number. When I meet other Franciscans, no matter how differently they're living the Franciscan life, I feel at home with them.

There is something of that feeling to this story. Mary is at a crisis point in her life, wrestling with the implications of the angel's message and living with the suspicions of those around her. She needs refuge and goes to stay with a member of her family, Elizabeth, who has also been visited by God. I imagine the two women spending many hours talking about what has happened to them and wondering how their unexpected pregnancies fit into God's plan. As descendants of Abraham, they shared in the blessings of God's chosen people and would have known the promise that 'in you all the families of the earth shall be blessed' (Genesis 12:3). Were their children to be the ones to bring this about? Was God fulfilling his promise in their day?

Jesus' family begins as everyone else's does, with a mother and father, aunts and uncles, but he is to draw into God's family all those who believe that there will be a fulfilment of what was spoken to us by the Lord.

Reflection

Is your family a place where you can speak of the things of God?

HJ CSF

In the Father's house

Now every year his [Jesus'] parents went to Jerusalem for the festival of the Passover. And when he was twelve years old, they went up as usual for the festival. When the festival was ended and they started to return, the boy Jesus stayed behind in Jerusalem, but his parents did not know it... After three days they found him in the temple... and his mother said to him, 'Child, why have you treated us like this? Look, your father and I have been searching for you in great anxiety.' He said to them, 'Why were you searching for me? Did you not know that I must be in my Father's house?'

After the birth stories, this is the next glimpse we have of Jesus. The apocryphal gospels (those not accepted into the Bible by the Church) have other stories, of Jesus working miracles as a child. It's natural to want more information about his formative years, but our first certain picture is this one.

It shows Jesus' parents as devout Jews, going up every year to Jerusalem for the Passover, taking Jesus with them. It is no accident that this story happens when he is twelve as that is the age at which Jewish boys make their bar mitzvah, taking on for themselves the responsibilities and obligations of the law. The nearest Christian equivalent would be confirmation.

Although the bar mitzvah as such is a later development, it is still likely that at the age of twelve there was a sense of childhood drawing to a close and Jesus, like any other child, is beginning to find his own way. His own way leads him like a homing pigeon to the temple, to the place of God's dwelling. There he joins the teachers and, in a pattern that we will see repeated in his relationship with his own disciples, sits among them, listening and asking questions.

In the dialogue with his parents, we can see something of the mutual bewilderment all parents and children experience as the child begins to separate, to find his own path, which to him seems obvious, but to his parents seems puzzling and even upsetting. Jesus' parents were not exempt from the problems faced by all parents of adolescents.

Prayer

Jesus, draw us to the Father's house with you.

HJ CSF

Going his own way

Then he [Jesus] went home; and the crowd came together again, so that they could not even eat. When his family heard it, they went out to restrain him, for people were saying, 'He has gone out of his mind.'... Then his mother and his brothers came; and standing outside, they sent to him and called him. A crowd was sitting around him; and they said to him, 'Your mother and your brothers and sisters are outside, asking for you.' And he replied, 'Who are my mother and my brothers?' And looking at those who sat around him, he said, 'Here are my mother and my brothers! Whoever does the will of God is my brother and sister and mother.'

We saw yesterday how Jesus was beginning to find his own path and how difficult that was for his parents. Today, we see an even starker example of puzzlement and perhaps even distress at the way in which he was living.

By now, his family could have been hoping that Jesus would have settled down, married and probably taken over Joseph's family business. Instead, at the age of about 30, he leaves home to wander around the countryside with a crowd of not very respectable disciples, getting into trouble with the authorities. In a society where family ties and expectations were very strong, this would have been shocking, so it's not surprising that people thought he had gone mad.

Jesus, though, chose to live by a different set of values and Mark reflects these in the way he writes his Gospel. Unlike Matthew, he has no genealogy and, unlike Luke, he has no birth stories and, unlike John, there is no poetic reflection on 'beginnings'. Rather, Mark begins with the adult Jesus being baptized by John and starting to proclaim the Kingdom. This story is the first appearance of his family and, despite being so close to him in one way, they obviously do not understand who he is or what his mission in life is.

We all hope that our families will understand and support us in our life choices, but sometimes they do not and perhaps cannot. Jesus experienced the pain of this lack of understanding and the need to find new circles of support for his new way of life.

Reflection
Where do you find support for your life of faith?

HJ CSF

Leaving everything

Peter began to say to him, 'Look, we have left everything and followed you.' Jesus said, 'Truly I tell you, there is no one who has left house or brothers or sisters or mother or father or children or fields, for my sake and for the sake of the good news, who will not receive a hundredfold now in this age—houses, brothers and sisters, mothers and children, and fields, with persecutions—and in the age to come eternal life. But many who are first will be last, and the last will be first.'

It was not only Jesus who had to make choices about whether to show allegiance to his birth family or a new and growing family of faith. Those who followed him had in some cases also been called to leave all that normally anchored them into the fabric of society—property, family ties, the agricultural life that underpinned their community—in order to do so.

This piece of dialogue follows immediately after Jesus talking about the difficulty of the rich entering the Kingdom and his descriptive image of the camel and the eye of the needle (vv. 23–27). He said these things in response to the man traditionally called the 'rich young ruler' who was challenged to 'sell what you own' and promised that 'you will have treasure in heaven' (v. 21).

In Jesus' response to Peter, however, even more is promised. There will be eternal life in 'the age to come', but there will also be far more than has been surrendered now, in this life and this age. This passage has often been seen as foundational to the religious life and a very good recruitment tool for it! Who would not be willing to give up what they have for the promise of a hundredfold more, as well as eternal life? Note, though, that there is also the promise of persecution—a sober estimation of the cost of the Kingdom.

Family is not to be an absolute priority for Jesus' disciples. For his sake and for the sake of his gospel, they may be called to leave it all and enter into a larger family of fellow disciples and a network of 'homes'.

Reflection

Have you ever had to choose between family and faith?

HJ CSF

Disturbing the peace

[Jesus said] 'Do not think that I have come to bring peace to the earth; I have not come to bring peace, but a sword. For I have come to set a man against his father, and a daughter against her mother, and a daughter-in-law against her mother-in-law; and one's foes will be members of one's own household. Whoever loves father or mother more than me is not worthy of me; and whoever loves son or daughter more than me is not worthy of me; and whoever does not take up the cross and follow me is not worthy of me. Those who find their life will lose it, and those who lose their life for my sake will find it.'

These words are some of the starkest and most challenging in the Gospels, but they do not come out of nowhere.

Those among Jesus' hearers who knew their own scriptures might well have recognized the words of verse 35 as echoing a prophecy of Micah's (7:6) 'the son treats the father with contempt, the daughter rises up against her mother'. These words were understood as being a prophecy of the messianic age and, in saying 'I have come', Jesus is identifying himself with this expectation and claiming that in his coming the prophecy is being fulfilled and, therefore, the woes that were seen as inaugurating the messianic age had also come.

The new work that God is doing in the coming of Jesus is so extraordinary that it is bound to cause terrible division—not just at the level of nations and religious institutions but also even at the heart of families. The sword that was to pierce Mary's soul (Luke 2:35) and divide his own family would also disturb the peace of many other households.

Nowhere does Jesus deny the value of family, nor that it is the normal context of life for most of his followers, but he does demand recognition of the priority of the call to follow him over even the most intimate of family ties. The love of Jesus must be at the very heart of the disciple's life, with all other loves taking their place around that central core.

Prayer

Lord Jesus, may I love you above all other people and things, and so be worthy to find my life in you.

HJ CSF

Paying attention to Jesus

Now as they went on their way, he [Jesus] entered a certain village, where a woman named Martha welcomed him into her home. She had a sister named Mary, who sat at the Lord's feet and listened to what he was saying. But Martha was distracted by her many tasks; so she came to him and asked, 'Lord, do you not care that my sister has left me to do all the work by myself? Tell her then to help me.' But the Lord answered her, 'Martha, Martha, you are worried and distracted by many things; there is need of only one thing. Mary has chosen the better part, which will not be taken away from her.'

Here is another story about putting Jesus at the centre, but this one has a rather less stark setting. Jesus is visiting a home that he knows well, one into which he is welcomed. We might also note that it is a home and family made up of two sisters and their brother. Welcoming and hospitable families can be of many kinds.

Jesus' apparent rejection of his own family did not mean that he never needed friendship or a sense of belonging. Although he taught that the demands of the kingdom must come first, he was fully human as well as fully divine, so needed the support of friends and family—however that family was defined—as we all do.

This story is often interpreted as one in which Jesus supports the contemplative life over and against the active one and he champions Mary and puts Martha down for her busyness. To many women in particular it has seemed a denigration of their daily commitment to keeping homes and families running smoothly.

In reality, however, Jesus does not put Martha and what she is doing down. Instead, he praises Mary because, at that particular moment, she has discerned that the most important activity is to listen to Jesus. She has perhaps seen that what he needs most is not food, but someone to hear him, to pay attention to what he is saying. That is the mark of a disciple, a member of Jesus' new family —we must be paying attention in each moment to what the Lord wants us to do, listening to his words.

Prayer

Lord, make me attentive to you today, ready to sit at your feet or serve you in action.

HJ CSF

United in one family

Then they returned to Jerusalem from the mount called Olivet, which is near Jerusalem, a sabbath day's journey away. When they had entered the city, they went to the room upstairs where they were staying, Peter, and John, and James, and Andrew, Philip and Thomas, Bartholomew and Matthew, James son of Alphaeus, and Simon the Zealot, and Judas son of James. All these were constantly devoting themselves to prayer, together with certain women, including Mary the mother of Jesus, as well as his brothers.

In these few verses from Luke's account of the time immediately after the ascension, there is a sense of redemption, that the apparently harsh way in which Jesus had treated his family is now being transformed. The list of apostles corresponds to Luke's list in his Gospel (6:14–16). These are the men who have been with him since the beginning of his ministry, becoming his new family, travelling with him and learning from him.

Now, at this crucial point in the very early life of the Church after the resurrection and the ascension, but before Pentecost and the coming of the Spirit, they are joined by others, by 'certain women', including Mary his mother, who had been given to the disciple whom Jesus loved (traditionally John) to be his mother and for the disciple to be her son (John 19:25–27). I wonder if Mary and Martha are also there, along with the women who were faithful in remaining at the cross when the disciples ran away.

Jesus' brothers and sisters are also there, even though they had thought him mad and been publicly rejected by him (Mark 3:19–21, 31–35). It would have been very easy for Jesus' natural family to resent his disciples, who had seemingly taken him away from them and apparently replaced them in his affections, but here they are, together, devoting themselves to prayer as they wait for the outpouring of the Spirit.

The two families have been united into one new family of faith. Those who might have seemed at odds have been drawn together by their shared faith in Jesus—their son, brother, friend, master.

Reflection

Does your own church family reflect this picture? Does it unite those who would naturally be at odds?

HJ CSF

Child of God

There is therefore now no condemnation for those who are in Christ Jesus. For the law of the Spirit of life in Christ Jesus has set you free from the law of sin and of death... For all who are led by the Spirit of God are children of God. For you did not receive the spirit of slavery to fall back into fear, but you have received a spirit of adoption. When we cry 'Abba! Father!' it is that very Spirit bearing witness with our spirit that we are children of God, and if children, then heirs, heirs of God and joint heirs with Christ—if, in fact, we suffer with him so that we may also be glorified with him.

When the Spirit came at Pentecost, it galvanized the disciples into preaching the word of God (Acts 2). It also changed how they saw themselves and understood their relationship with God.

In this section of the letter to the Romans, Paul contrasts the way of life with the way of death. Contrary to what many think of Paul, this is not primarily about morality; it is about relationship. What the coming of the Spirit makes possible is a new relationship with God, a relationship that changes things now and promises more for the future.

The indwelling Spirit transforms us from slaves into beloved children, removing the condemnation that we formally bore and adopting us into God's family as children and heirs. This is possible because we come to share in what Jesus has done, suffering with him so that we may also be glorified with him and become heirs with him.

In Jewish law, two witnesses were needed to establish the truth and here the two witnesses are the Spirit and the individual Christian. The new law is not about sin and death, but life, freedom from fear, adoption now and the promise of inheriting with Christ all that he has made possible through his cross and resurrection.

This will be seen in our lives because of the intimacy with which we address God, sharing in the cry of 'Abba' that was Jesus' own.

Reflection

What does it mean to you to be a child of God?

HJ CSF

Our brother Jesus

It was fitting that God, for whom and through whom all things exist, in bringing many children to glory, should make the pioneer of their salvation perfect through sufferings. For the one who sanctifies and those who are sanctified all have one Father. For this reason Jesus is not ashamed to call them brothers and sisters, saying, 'I will proclaim your name to my brothers and sisters, in the midst of the congregation I will praise you.' And again, 'I will put my trust in him.' And again, 'Here am I and the children whom God has given me.'

If we can, with Jesus, call God 'Abba'—Father—then it follows that we can also know ourselves to be brothers and sisters of Jesus. This was a truth that never ceased to astonish Francis of Assisi. In his 'Letter to the Faithful', he wrote, 'Oh, how holy and how loving, pleasing, humble, peaceful, sweet, lovable, and desirable above all things to have such a Brother and such a Son: our Lord Jesus Christ, Who gave up His life for His sheep' (*Francis and Clare: The complete works*, Paulist Press, 1982, pp. 63–4).

The word 'pioneer' in secular literature was used of the founder and protector of a city and could also mean the head of a family or a clan. In the New Testament, it is used of Jesus in our passage above and in Hebrews 12:2 (also translated 'pioneer'), Acts 3:15 (translated 'Author') and 5:31 (translated 'Leader'). In the Old Testament, where it is found in Exodus 6:14

and Numbers 10:4, it has the added nuance of a leader who goes in front of those he leads. So, Jesus, our pioneer, has brought those whom he leads to salvation by going ahead of them and enduring suffering and death.

We are included in God's family as children of the Father and brothers and sisters of Jesus not through our own work, but because of God's work in the life and death of Jesus and because Jesus, through his grace, is pleased to share with us the fruits of his life and death. It is a pure gift. No wonder Francis marvelled at it.

Prayer

Abba, thank you for making me your child and giving me Jesus as a brother.

HJ CSF

Questions, questions

He [Jesus] left that place and came to his home town, and his disciples followed him. On the sabbath he began to teach in the synagogue, and many who heard him were astounded. They said, 'Where did this man get all this? What is this wisdom that has been given to him? What deeds of power are being done by his hands! Is not this the carpenter, the son of Mary and brother of James and Joses and Judas and Simon, and are not his sisters here with us?' And they took offence at him.

Jesus' neighbours took offence at him and this passage has continued to offend and perplex ever since.

Two main questions arise. How could Jesus be the Messiah if his own people, who lived in expectation of the Messiah, had rejected him? If Mary, his mother, as many Christians believe, remained a virgin for life, how can Jesus have had brothers and sisters?

The rejection of Jesus by the people in his home town perhaps makes some sense if we think about how hard it can be to hear the wisdom of those who are close to us. Most preachers dread preaching to their own family and certainly, in my community, we feel that preaching to our own Franciscan sisters is quite daunting. They know us too well and can compare our words on Sunday with how we are on Monday morning!

Perhaps there was also a sense that the Messiah could not come from people like them. We too readily underestimate God's capacity to use the apparently ordinary and mundane in his work.

Today, many parts of the Church celebrate a feast in honour of the Virgin Mary. The theology of the perpetual virginity of Mary hadn't yet been formulated when Mark wrote his Gospel. Later writers explained the existence of brothers and sisters in various ways. Perhaps they were children of Joseph by a previous marriage or cousins or, in fact, Mary and Joseph had them later. We have no way of knowing. What really matters is that Mary, by giving her consent to God, gave flesh to God and made possible the extension of Jesus' family to include all who believed, then and now.

Reflection

What place does Mary have in your spiritual life?

HJ CSF

All one in Christ

But now that faith has come, we are no longer subject to a disciplinarian, for in Christ Jesus you are all children of God through faith. As many of you as were baptized into Christ have clothed yourselves with Christ. There is no longer Jew or Greek, there is no longer slave or free, there is no longer male and female; for all of you are one in Christ Jesus. And if you belong to Christ, then you are Abraham's offspring, heirs according to the promise.

God's new family is radically new. Those who are now to be found 'in Christ Jesus' by sharing in his life and death through baptism are intimately bound up with him. Julian of Norwich puts it beautifully: 'He is our clothing that, for love, wrappeth us up and windeth us about; embraceth us... for tender love' (*The Revelations of Divine Love of Julian of Norwich*, James Walsh (trans.), Burns & Oates, 1961, p. 53).

Just as our clothes do not obliterate our identity, neither does our being clothed in Christ—we are still ourselves in all our glorious diversity. What has changed is that our differences are not to be used as reasons for division. Jew and Greek, slave and free, male and female, were some of the major distinctions between people in Jesus' time, but we can think of latter-day equivalents. Paul writes that, as we are 'children of God through faith', these distinctions no longer matter because our identity in Christ overrides what would otherwise divide us. As he writes to the Ephesians, 'For he is our peace; in his flesh he... has broken down the dividing wall' (2:14).

Thus, we have a new identity and it goes right back to where we began these notes, in the genealogy of Jesus, tracing his line back to Abraham. The promise made by God to Abraham (Genesis 17:1–8), fulfilled first in Christ himself, has now been extended to the whole Church. We have been brought into the covenant, into the family of Abraham, into the wonderful promises of God. It does not stop there—we are called to draw others into this radically new family, where all can belong.

Reflection

Has any of what you have read this fortnight changed how you think about yourself in relation to Jesus, your own family and the family of the Church?

HJ CSF

We've got problems!

Grace and peace to you from God our Father and the Lord Jesus Christ. I always thank God for you because of his grace given you in Christ Jesus. For in him you have been enriched in every way—in all your speaking and in all your knowledge—because our testimony about Christ was confirmed in you. Therefore you do not lack any spiritual gift as you eagerly wait for our Lord Jesus Christ to be revealed. He will keep you strong to the end, so that you will be blameless on the day of our Lord Jesus Christ. God, who has called you into fellowship with his Son Jesus Christ our Lord, is faithful.

There were some significant problems in the Corinthian part of the Church. The Christians there knew this and so does Paul. The difference between them seems to be that Paul knows their nature (and solution) whereas the Corinthians don't.

In the early chapters of his letter, Paul establishes fundamental truths and basic issues because, if these are ignored, there is little chance of sorting out the problems. He begins by reminding the Corinthians that, because of Jesus, they know God's grace and their lives are enriched in every way. They have received spiritual gifts for public ministry and their private relationship with God is safeguarded by the faithfulness of Christ. In other words, if there are problems (and there are) then they are not coming from God's direction!

Paul is gently second-guessing the Corinthians to make sure that his letter isn't received with a self-righteous , 'Well! None of this is my fault!' He knows only too well how our fallen human nature leads us to blame others and even God for the problems that beset us. Adam and Eve did it in the Garden of Eden, the Christians in Corinth did it and so do we.

When Paul reminds us that God is gracious, forgiving and faithful, he does so for a reason. Even Christians need to be reminded of what, so often, we are not! As long as we remember that, we are less likely to blame others (or God) for the problems we have created ourselves. We are probably also more readily going to ask for forgiveness.

Prayer

Lord, forgive me for shifting the blame when the problem lies with me.

DR

1 CORINTHIANS 1:10–13 (NIV)

Divided

I appeal to you, brothers and sisters, in the name of our Lord Jesus Christ, that all of you agree with one another so that there may be no divisions among you and that you may be perfectly united in mind and thought. My dear friends, some from Chloe's household have informed me that there are quarrels among you. What I mean is this: One of you says, 'I follow Paul'; another, 'I follow Apollos'; another, 'I follow Cephas'; still another, 'I follow Christ.' Is Christ divided?

This passage famously allows Christians to pat themselves on the back while declaring with modest confidence, 'Well, at least our church isn't like that!' Usually, the thought of any single church splitting itself with such internal rivalry fills us with astonishment. The 'internal division' in Corinth, though, may not have been quite as we imagine.

Archaeologists tell us that buildings of this time were limited in size due to both materials and techniques. Most large gatherings were conducted in the open air because even the homes of the wealthy only had rooms of a size sufficient to host about 50 people at once. This being the case, if the church in Corinth had, say, 200 members, they had to meet either outside or in groups of 50 or so with different 'patrons' that the members themselves chose (Paul, Apollos, Cephas, Christ).

This passage is therefore not about division within a single congregation but about how the church can preserve its unity across a whole town. If this passage were updated, it might read, 'One of you says, "I'm an Anglican"; another, "I'm a Methodist"; another, "I'm a Baptist"; still another, "I'm United Reformed." Is Christ divided?'

A church can meet in different venues and still be united or else it can split. It's all down to what we think of Christ and each other. Recognizing that *Jesus* is the head of the Church, not the leaders, and 'other groups' belong to him just as much as we do is the foundation of unity. Remembering that we (fallen human beings) tend to be competitive for all the wrong reasons ensures that we build the Church carefully. Admitting this to Jesus and one another makes it possible to demolish that which should never have been built at all.

Prayer

Lord Jesus, may I be one with other believers, an answer to your prayer (see John 17:20–21).

DR

Wise or foolish?

For since in the wisdom of God the world through its wisdom did not know him, God was pleased through the foolishness of what was preached to save those who believe. Jews demand miraculous signs and Greeks look for wisdom, but we preach Christ crucified: a stumbling block to Jews and foolishness to Gentiles, but to those whom God has called, both Jews and Greeks, Christ the power of God and the wisdom of God. For the foolishness of God is wiser than human wisdom, and the weakness of God is stronger than human strength.

This passage sounds very grand and its sonorous words, 'wisdom' and 'foolishness', echo in our ears. The word Paul chooses for 'worldly wisdom', though, carries overtones of 'show-off', which punctures the grandeur a little.

It's another facet of our fallen human nature that we love to be right and how we go about proving that is culturally conditioned. Here, Paul says that Jews look for miraculous back-up while Greeks compose enormously complicated theories. The aim of each, though, is the same: we want to prove how right we are. We look at what God has said and done and shake our heads in disbelief. How ridiculous that God should take on human form in Jesus Christ and then be crucified! How weak! How foolish! How irrelevant! As Paul says, however, this is God's 'foolishness' and it shows up our human 'wisdom' as being nothing of the kind.

When we look at a problem and say to God, 'If I were you, I'd do it like this', our 'wisdom' is revealed as original sin. It leads us to roll up our sleeves, elbow God out of the way and work things out without him. Unless our solution contains the 'foolishness' of God, our 'wisdom' is simply boastful showing off.

So far, in the first 25 verses of his letter, Paul has highlighted some potential errors in the workings of the Corinthian church. If they are trying to address their problems by blaming God, looking to leaders or seeking human solutions, then nothing much will change. Unless they sort out their errors, they will have little hope of addressing their problems. Paul is reminding them to stop looking for solutions and start seeking the true wisdom of God.

Reflection

*God's solution is a person,
not a programme.*

DR

As you were

Brothers and sisters, think of what you were when you were called. Not many of you were wise by human standards; not many were influential; not many were of noble birth. But God chose the foolish things of the world to shame the wise; God chose the weak things of the world to shame the strong. He chose the lowly things of this world and the despised things—and the things that are not—to nullify the things that are, so that no one may boast before him. It is because of him that you are in Christ Jesus, who has become for us wisdom from God—that is, our righteousness, holiness and redemption. Therefore, as it is written: 'Let those who boast boast in the Lord.'

It's an astonishing truth that, in Christ, everyone is equal. The prince and the pauper stand shoulder to shoulder before God's throne and those who are reborn of their heavenly father are siblings. In the kingdom of God, no one stands higher than anyone else because all are dependent on Christ.

It's a less astonishing truth that, in the Church, the human way of hierarchy has a habit of re-emerging! This happens because every church around the world is filled not with sin-free, saintly people, but sinful, forgiven saints. The Church is a work in progress that rarely progresses in a straight line. That the Corinthian church had problems is just another way of saying that it contained people! In these verses, Paul is reminding the Corinthians where they came from and what Jesus did for them. He is addressing another potential error and another facet of fallen humanity—the desire to lord it over one another. However, those who pride themselves on their wisdom, influence and nobility set themselves up as competitors to God and will be shown to be unrighteous, unholy and unredeemed. God chooses to work with, and through, the foolish, weak, lowly and despised, which (Paul gently points out) describes the Corinthians themselves.

In 21st-century terms, if the Corinthians are going to tackle their problems, then they will need to do so from a position of honest self-awareness. The biblical term for this is, of course, humility.

Prayer

Lord, may I always remember who I am and never forget who you are.

DR

God in us

When I came to you, brothers and sisters, I did not come with eloquence or superior wisdom as I proclaimed to you the testimony about God. For I resolved to know nothing while I was with you except Jesus Christ and him crucified. I came to you in weakness and fear, and with much trembling. My message and my preaching were not with wise and persuasive words, but with a demonstration of the Spirit's power, so that your faith might not rest on human wisdom, but on God's power.

I suppose that most of us have some kind of mental picture of Paul. We probably think of him as a hero, striding fearlessly into every situation, stirring up trouble and being a right pain at times. Interestingly, whenever Paul describes himself, he comes over as timid and resigned to having to struggle. So, was he a mighty man or, to some extent, weak and ineffectual? The answer seems to be 'both'.

In all of his letters, Paul reveals a self-awareness of who he is and what he has been. He never glosses over his past or present sin, his personal failings. He is also just as aware of who Jesus is and what the Spirit is doing in his life. So, is he weak? Apparently, yes. Is he a mighty man? Definitely, yes, because of God's Spirit within him.

At this point in his letter, Paul reminds the Corinthians that he is no different from them. He is not trying to pull rank so that they fall into line. Instead, his desire is to stand alongside them and point them in the right direction, which is the same as it has always been—towards Jesus Christ crucified. Through the cross, their lives have been put right and their current problems will be put right in the same way.

The process they face now is no different from the process they have already experienced. They will need to admit fault, seek forgiveness and submit to the Spirit. Guarded and guided by the Spirit, their problems will be solved even if they, like Paul, quail at the thought of what they must confront. If they look to God, they will rise, mightily, to the challenge.

Reflection

God's commission is always a co-mission—him and us together.

DR

Mature thinking

We do, however, speak a message of wisdom among the mature, but not the wisdom of this age or of the rulers of this age, who are coming to nothing. No, we speak of God's secret wisdom, a wisdom that has been hidden and that God destined for our glory before time began. None of the rulers of this age understood it, for if they had, they would not have crucified the Lord of glory. However, as it is written: 'No eye has seen, no ear has heard, no mind has conceived what God has prepared for those who love him'—but God has revealed it to us by his Spirit.

The words the 'rulers of this age' may refer to spiritual beings, human leaders or both. Given the context, though, Paul may also be thinking of his old companions mentioned in Philippians 3:5 who are now the religious leaders of his own people. Paul was a rising star when Jesus met him on the road to Damascus and changed his life. Since then, there must have been occasions when the persecution Paul suffered was meted out by old schoolfriends.

In that same Philippians passage, Paul goes on to share how he has learned that being a ruler is worth nothing (v. 8). He has left that life behind and has no intention of re-establishing another version of it in the Church. In this passage, he reminds the Corinthians that neither should they. To rule is to usurp the role of God, which is to sin, which caused Christ to be crucified. Yet, in the death of Jesus, God has hidden his wisdom, which is forgiveness and new life. Thus, the crucifixion, which was caused by sin, becomes the solution to sin.

Again and again, Paul is captivated by the simple complexity of what God has done, but he never gets so caught up in the theory that he forgets the 'why'. God is motivated by love and Paul responds to that love by being obedient to God's call. Paul was a theologian who lived out his theology.

In these verses, he is preparing the way for a mature approach to problem-solving. If the Corinthians' problems are of mountainous proportions, they will need a theological base camp from which they can make a practical attempt on the summit.

Reflection

If I ruled the world… I'd be God.

DR

Spirituality

The Spirit searches all things, even the deep things of God. For who knows the thoughts of another human being except that person's own spirit within? In the same way no one knows the thoughts of God except the Spirit of God. We have not received the spirit of the world but the Spirit who is from God, that we may understand what God has freely given us.

The word 'spirituality' is widely used in our culture to mean anything pertaining to the spirit. It makes sense to us because we define ourselves, as did the ancient Greeks, as consisting of body, mind and spirit. Anything that is not to do with the body or mind is, by default, 'spiritual'. As a result of this body, mind and spirit division, the idea of a holistic integration of the three has become increasingly popular.

In contrast to this, Paul, the other apostles and Jesus himself were all working within a Hebrew understanding of self. It did not differentiate between aspects of the self, simply between good and bad. According to their thinking, a person was just 'me' in this life (and the next), so spirituality did not concern them, only righteousness.

In this passage, when Paul writes about a man's spirit knowing his own thoughts, he is not describing one aspect of the man examining another, but of a unified being knowing himself. Thus, the Spirit of God is not one aspect of God, but

God in every sense and, in Paul's understanding, when God shares his Spirit with human beings, he is sharing himself completely.

This Hebrew understanding of self sheds light on what the New Testament writers thought was happening in Jesus' incarnation. Jesus was not an aspect of God, but God himself (see John 1:1; Colossians 2:9). It also explains why, for Paul, there was no division between theology and practical Christian living.

The Corinthians, however, were Greek, so there are two questions to ask with regard to the problems they were facing (with power, wealth and sexual morality). First, to what extent did their problems arise from their divided understanding of self? Second, to what extent does our own culture stumble at the same hurdles and for the same reason?

Prayer

Thank you, Holy Spirit, that, in knowing you, I know Jesus and my heavenly Father.

DR

Christian spirituality

This is what we speak, not in words taught us by human wisdom but in words taught by the Spirit, expressing spiritual truths in spiritual words. The man without the Spirit does not accept the things that come from the Spirit of God, for they are foolishness to him, and he cannot understand them, because they are spiritually discerned. The spiritual man makes judgments about all things, but he himself is not subject to any man's judgment: 'For who has known the mind of the Lord that he may instruct him?' But we have the mind of Christ.

Paul uses a word here that the Corinthians, with their Greek background, understood readily—'spiritual'. He redefines it for them, though, as meaning the byproduct of the presence of the Spirit of God in their lives. As Christians, they are a new creation (2 Corinthians 5:17) and it is therefore appropriate for them to express themselves in a new language, as it were—one that is taught to them by the Holy Spirit, the language of spirituality.

Until the Corinthians became Christian believers, Paul preached to them only the message of Christ crucified. In his thinking, repentance, forgiveness, baptism and the indwelling Spirit had to come first. 'Spiritual conversation', as they would think of it, came later, among those who already 'have the mind of Christ'.

In this passage, he reminds the Corinthians of their mutual dependence on God. He wants them to listen to the Spirit, confident that they will hear the words he says to them. Once they have heard God's words, then they will be able to make proper judgments about the problems they face. In this way, Paul makes it clear to the Corinthians that they must seek a spiritual solution and he trusts them to do this because they are spiritual people—Christians who have received the Spirit of God.

In our own time it's worth comparing Paul's approach with our own. How often do we look for spirituality in those who hold different faiths or none, but forget to mention the cross to them? How often do we ignore the spirituality of Christian people and use secular solutions to solve church problems? Just how similar to the Corinthians are we?

Prayer

Thank you for giving me your Spirit. Help me to understand your mind.

DR

Spiritual maturity

Brothers and sister, I could not address you as spiritual but as worldly—mere infants in Christ. I gave you milk, not solid food, for you were not yet ready for it. Indeed, you are still not ready. You are still worldly. For since there is jealousy and quarrelling among you, are you not worldly? Are you not acting like mere human beings? For when one says, 'I follow Paul,' and another, 'I follow Apollos,' are you not mere human beings?

The Corinthian church regarded itself as a success story. Initially under the leadership of Paul, Aquila, Priscilla, Silas, Timothy and Apollos, it became a thriving fellowship, continuing under local leaders after the apostle's departure. The church met regularly to worship and the gifts of the Spirit were powerfully evident. It was the kind of church that, if it existed today, would be regarded by many as a role model.

Paul's opinion of the church is, clearly, rather different. He points out that when they first believed, their immaturity confined his teaching to 'spiritual milk'. They were worldly, riddled with the ambitions of fallen humanity and unable to engage with 'meaty' issues. Have they now matured? Hardly! By Paul's standards they haven't changed at all. They are just as immature and worldly as they ever were and their behaviour proves it.

This, again, shows how Paul is using the concept of 'spirituality'. He doesn't mean ideas understood, words spoken, concepts grasped or spiritual gifts exercised. Spirituality is about behaving our faith, about being Christian. Those who are spiritually mature behave in a certain way: they are humble about their faults, encourage each other, listen to the Spirit and sacrifice themselves for the sake of others.

Spiritual maturity is about being Christ-like, denying the self, picking up our cross each day and living as Jesus lived (Luke 9:23). Until we receive the Spirit, we are unable to live like this, but the indwelling Spirit changes us. Therefore, says Paul, the way Christians behave demonstrates the presence (or absence) of the Spirit and shows them to be either spiritual or unspiritual. Today, we would phrase it differently as 'You talk the talk, but are you walking the walk?'

Reflection
The only role model for Christians is Jesus.

DR

Partners in ministry

What, after all, is Apollos? And what is Paul? Only servants, through whom you came to believe—as the Lord has assigned to each his task. I planted the seed, Apollos watered it, but God made it grow. So neither the one who plants nor the one who waters is anything, but only God, who makes things grow. The one who plants and the one who waters have one purpose, and they will each be rewarded according to their own labour. For we are God's fellow workers; you are God's field, God's building.

When a church advertises for a new minister, it produces a 'person specification'. This might be a list of the previous minister's strengths or strengths the church wishes the previous minister had had! Often, though, the specification is all-embracing and the church expects the new minister to plough, plant, water, weed, scare crows, tend, debug, harvest, thresh, mill, bake, serve, clear away and wash up. The general feeling is that, if the new minister can do everything, then the church will be successful.

Paul, interestingly, seems to hold a different view of ministry. He knows his gifts and gets on with exercising them. He sees gifts in others and expects them to do the same. That's why the Corinthian church was established by Paul, Aquila, Priscilla, Timothy, Silas and Apollos and it's what we, today, call collaborative ministry.

Talent and collaboration are different. The former requires a top person who runs everything and the latter doesn't. In Paul's thinking, neither he nor any of the others are 'top people'. The only top person is Jesus and everyone is a fellow worker with him. According to Paul, the Corinthians are making a fundamental error when they try to create a new hierarchy under their leaders because the church has only one tier of hierarchy—God at the top and everyone else submitting to him. Astonishingly, in Christ, God steps down even from this top position and descends to the bottom that all may be raised up (John 6:38–40).

In some churches, the departure of the minister is regarded as a disaster. This may indicate a Corinthian view of ministry where human leaders are overly important. After all, Jesus, the Lord of the Church, hasn't gone anywhere.

Reflection

One faith, one Church, one Lord.

DR

Judgment day

By the grace God has given me, I laid a foundation as an expert builder, and someone else is building on it. But each one should build with care. For no one can lay any foundation other than the one already laid, which is Jesus Christ. If anyone builds on this foundation using gold, silver, costly stones, wood, hay or straw, that peson's work will be shown for what it is, because the Day will bring it to light. It will be revealed with fire, and the fire will test the quality of everyone's work. If the building survives, the builder will receive a reward. If it is burned up, the builder will suffer loss; the builder, however, will be saved, but only as one escaping through the flames.

This passage refers to two aspects of judgment day. First, it applies to individual Christian lives—to those who have accepted the 'foolishness' of the cross, been blessed by the grace of God and empowered by his Spirit. These people will be saved because their lives rest on Christ and he is the foundation of all that they are. The question is, though, is he the foundation of all that they do as well as what they believe in their hearts? Kind actions and gentle deeds are like bricks made of precious jewels and those who do this are building a life in Christ that has eternal value and will survive being tested. Second, the passage can be applied to ministry. Sacrificial service and sharing the gospel are also 'precious bricks' that build God's kingdom in a way that has lasting value.

Private lives and public ministries are, inevitably, a mixture of the good, the bad and the ugly! Alongside every precious brick there will be other bricks made from selfishness, disobedience and sin. Everyone (including God) wishes that they weren't there, but they are and, in this life, individual Christians and churches exhibit the sublime right next to the repulsive. At judgment, however, while the foundation remains, everything else is tested. This is true for Paul, Apollos, the Corinthian church, us and our own local churches. How much will survive judgment day? Only God knows and what he counts as valuable is often not what we expect (Matthew 25:37–40).

Prayer

Lord Jesus, please teach me to discern what is precious to you.

DR

True wisdom

Don't you know that you yourselves are God's temple and that God's Spirit lives in you? If anyone destroys God's temple, God will destroy that person; for God's temple is sacred, and you are that temple. Do not deceive yourselves. If any of you think you are wise by the standards of this age, you should become 'fools' so that you may become wise. For the wisdom of this world is foolishness in God's sight... So then, no more boasting about human leaders! All things are yours, whether Paul or Apollos or Cephas or the world or life or death or the present or the future—all are yours, and you are of Christ, and Christ is of God.

This passage can be applied to an individual or a church, but Paul's original intention was to address the Corinthian Christians as a body. Just as the temple in Jerusalem was regarded as the place where God dwelt (in the most holy place, behind the inner curtain), so now the indwelling Holy Spirit makes the church 'God's temple'. Each individual Corinthian is a brick in this new, spiritual temple and, therefore, the quality of each life matters—and there is no excuse because God has given himself to Christ and Christ has given himself to them.

There is a macro and a micro version of the same truth here. Jesus, who is the foundation of the Church, is also the foundation of each life/brick that makes up the Church. The Spirit who gives life to the temple also gives life to every individual who is built into it. In Jesus, God the Father has 'fool-ishly' expressed his holy and eternal love in the human realm of sin and mortality.

This, says Paul, is the wisdom of God, but, unfortunately, there are people who don't agree with it. They want to do things differently—in effect, they want to destroy God's temple. Clearly, Paul could be talking about those who persecute the Church, but, actually, he is talking about its members—those who apply secular standards and solutions (the wisdom of this world) to the problems facing the community of believers.

The Church, he says, is founded on God, given life by God and ruled by God. The only appropriate solutions, therefore, are God's.

Prayer

Dear God, thank you that your Spirit dwells in me.

DR

Fear not

So then, you ought to regard us as servants of Christ and as those entrusted with the secret things of God. Now it is required that those who have been given a trust must prove faithful. I care very little if I am judged by you or by any human court; indeed, I do not even judge myself. My conscience is clear, but that does not make me innocent. It is the Lord who judges me. Therefore judge nothing before the appointed time; wait till the Lord comes. He will bring to light what is hidden in darkness and will expose the motives of people's hearts. At that time each will receive praise from God.

So far in his letter, Paul has talked about the divisions within the Corinthian church and addressed the fundamental issues of true wisdom and real spirituality. These come from, and rest on, God. Some church members, however, have taken on themselves the task of defining what is wise and spiritual. This is original sin—our fallen human nature leading us to set ourselves up in place of God.

Having introduced the subject of judgment, though, Paul is determined that this shouldn't go the same way as wisdom and spirituality. He does not want the Corinthians to read his letter and begin their own witch hunt! It is not their place to judge. In contemporary terms, Paul is telling the church to draw a line under what's happened and move on. It doesn't matter who did what (and to whom) to create the current situation. God will judge and that's all that matters. Their task is to repent, seek God in sincere faith and do whatever God tells them to do.

We tend to fear judgment, but Paul doesn't. He knows that every Christian life, and every church, (including his own), is a mixture of jewels and rubbish. He also knows that, at judgment, not only will the rubbish be burned away, the jewels will be left. Everyone, he says, will receive God's praise, so don't try to second-guess God, but be content to wait for his verdict—it comes from the same God who has given himself for and to us. Why would his judgment be anything but loving?

Reflection

Do not be afraid. I bring you good news of great joy (Luke 2:10).

DR

1 Corinthians 4:6–7, 10–13 (NIV, abridged)

Scum of the earth?

Now, brothers and sisters, I have applied these things to myself and Apollos for your benefit, so that you may learn from us the meaning of the saying, 'Do not go beyond what is written.' Then you will not take pride in one over against another. For who makes you different from anyone else? What do you have that you did not receive? And if you did receive it, why do you boast as though you did not? ... We are fools for Christ, but you are so wise in Christ! We are weak, but you are strong! You are honoured, we are dishonoured! To this very hour we go hungry and thirsty, we are in rags, we are brutally treated, we are homeless. We work hard with our own hands. When we are cursed, we bless; when we are persecuted, we endure it... Up to this moment we have become the scum of the earth, the refuse of the world.

Paul now draws comparisons between his own understanding of what it is to be Christian and the Corinthians' concept of Christianity. The differences go something like this. Paul is a well-to-do religious leader who gave up everything to serve Christ. He exchanged a comfortable life for one of persecution and the wisdom he had been taught for the foolishness of the cross. He sought to live a holy life in the face of adversity and was hated for it. The Corinthians, however, have got the idea that God elevates Christians above other people. They have exchanged lowly lives for status in the Church and revel in the honour they receive from fellow believers when they exercise leadership.

The final difference is this. The Corinthians have based their ideas on the 'wisdom of this world' (3:19) and, to do so, they have gone beyond God's word. Paul, on the other hand, has applied God's actual words to his life. This also highlights the one similarity between the Corinthians and himself—everything that applies to Paul applies to them and their lives should look like his!

It's worth considering which gospel we preach ourselves. Is it Paul's—one of sacrificial self-giving in response to the self-giving of God—or is it the Corinthian's—become a Christian, look at the benefits!

Prayer

Dear Lord Jesus, please give me the strength to shoulder my cross and follow only you.

DR

Imitate me

I am not writing this to shame you, but to warn you, as my dear children. Even though you have ten thousand guardians in Christ, you do not have many fathers, for in Christ Jesus I became your father through the gospel. Therefore I urge you to imitate me. For this reason I am sending to you Timothy, my son whom I love, who is faithful in the Lord. He will remind you of my way of life in Christ Jesus, which agrees with what I teach everywhere in every church… I will come to you very soon if the Lord is willing.

In our culture, we tend to say, 'This is what I believe—what do you think about it?' We expect debate and hope that, at some point, other people will come around to our point of view. We may even, deep down, have doubts about whether our ideas are right or not and may therefore find it easier to cope with others' rejection, rather than their acceptance.

Paul is not only a man from another culture but also someone who has experienced a relationship with Jesus Christ for a very long time. The hallmark of all his teaching is that he points people, first, to the crucified Christ and then encourages them to accept the living presence of God's Spirit.

Paul is almost ready to tackle the problems specific to the Corinthian church, but, before he does, there is one more fundamental issue to address. He intends to visit them, but, in the meantime, Timothy will return to Corinth and make it absolutely clear that what Paul is teaching is not some sort of personal agenda or weird hypothesis. The letter contains the truth as it is agreed by all the churches.

Paul's ideas are often complex but they are never abstract because they describe a person—Jesus—not a theory. This letter may be studied by academics today, but it was written for the benefit of ordinary people, living in a culture not dissimilar to our own. Paul's expectation is that his readers will seek Jesus Christ and find him, so he urges his readers to imitate him because that's what he does himself—seeks his Lord and finds him.

Prayer

Lord, may I be faithful to you always.

DR

The BRF
Magazine

Richard Fisher writes...

Discipleship was never meant to be a lonely affair. At BRF, we understand the importance of partnership in our spiritual journey: we see its benefits in our work every day as people with a variety of skills and giftings come together to further our ministry. We are also constantly aware of the support we receive from those of you who pray regularly for us—thank you!

Many of you will already know that BRF moved premises in August 2007, and a short report on the move (see page 142) gives you a taste of the excitement we all feel about this new stage in the organization's life. We look forward to developing links with local churches and schools here as time goes on.

Before that, in this issue of the *BRF Magazine*, Sharon Durant outlines the advantages of using *Foundations21*, BRF's web-based discipleship resource, along with others in your church. If you haven't already done so, why not start a group that can share insights and encourage one another to learn and develop from this innovative programme?

We've also chosen four books to bring to your attention in this issue. Naomi recommends *Six Men—Encountering God*, a page-turning collection of real-life testimonies. As Naomi mentions, the witness of Christians is key to each story, showing how we can help

people on to the path of discipleship even before they affirm a faith in Jesus. *Seeking Faith, Finding God*, her second recommendation, encourages us to keep asking questions about faith, and would be an ideal book to study together in a small group.

There are also extracts from *The Fourfold Leadership of Jesus*, essential reading for those whose full-time calling is about enabling other people to become better disciples, and *Footsteps to the Feast*, a book of special events tailor-made to help children enjoy the festivals of the church year. Our extract from this book is from the chapter on Trinity—a reminder, if we needed it, that partnership is at the very heart of the Godhead.

Don't go it alone! Let BRF encourage you to find new ways of joining with others in your journey of discipleship.

Richard Fisher, Chief Executive

What's ongoing and what's going on in your church?

Foundations21
THE NEW WAY TO DO DISCIPLESHIP

Sharon Durant

At first glance, there's not much difference between the phrases 'ongoing' and 'going on', but there is a subtle distinction, which you can clearly see if you look through my notes from office meetings. I often report to my colleagues that something is 'ongoing', meaning I should have done it but haven't got round to it yet. But I wouldn't say that the job was 'going on', because that would imply that I had actually done something about it!

Of course, we also use the word 'ongoing' for the routine parts of our lives that happen regularly over a long stretch of time. Conversely, we talk of things that are 'going on' to mean the events and situations that are taking up our immediate attention.

Discipleship is an ongoing aspect of the church's mandate, but is it going on? Is it really happening and connecting with where people are at the moment—or is discipleship being brushed under the carpet as something mundane and routine, something we might look at when we have more time?

> *Discipleship … not just 'ongoing' but really going on*

Thinking of the church where I worship, the regular programme of home groups provides an opportunity for ongoing discipleship week-by-week; but at 10pm, when we wash up the coffee cups and head back out to everyday life, sometimes I tick 'discipleship' off my list and forget about actively pursuing my faith until the next meeting rolls around.

In using *Foundations21* with others in your church, discipleship can be something that is not just 'ongoing' but really going on and bringing the journey of faith into the centre of the church's activity.

As an individual, you can follow

a pathway through *Foundations21*, exploring twelve key aspects of the Christian faith. With much of the content accessed through your computer and the Internet, you can log on and continue your discipleship at home, at work or even on the train if there's a WiFi connection. Each 'waymarker' you pass plots your progress through *Foundations21* and, consequently, a milestone in your journey of faith.

You can easily take a year (or more) on the material found within *Foundations21*, spending a month looking at each of the topics: God the Father, Jesus, the Holy Spirit, the Cross and Resurrection, Church, the Bible, Prayer, Worship, Intimacy with God, Christian Lifestyle, Christian Ministry and Christian Mission.

With four different learning styles, suited to different personalities, you can explore the rich content of *Foundations21* in a way that suits you and complements other members of the group. Some people use the same learning style throughout; others first use the learning style that best suits them, then take different approaches to the material to look at the topic from a fresh perspective.

Foundations21 is an engrossing experience and all the more fulfilling if you can share the excitement of your faith with like-minded people. Each day there are 'daily deliveries' of Bible passages, Psalms, inspirational thoughts and scripture promises. I have found that when something strikes me as profound, it is easy to share that thought with a friend by email or note it in my *Foundations21* journal for further reflection.

In the course of exploring the learning aspect of discipleship, *Foundations21* links to over 7500 thematically similar articles from external websites. This gives individuals the chance to study at their own level, ponder the personal challenges God may be raising in their lives and share those challenges with a mentor or with the group, which provides the support we all need to grow in our faith.

Each person explores a different avenue and takes their own unique path

As a *Foundations21* group, church members draw support from each other—but not just to keep going. A wide range of opinions and insights can be drawn upon as each person explores a different avenue and takes their own unique path through *Foundations21*. The simple question 'What has God been teaching you through *Foundations21*?' can start a whole evening's discussion and prayer as each person shares from their own experience and the way God has been speaking to them.

Each person has a part to play in the church, however small it may seem, and in the wider world. *Foundations21* enables churches to discover each individual's role in mission and ministry, looking at how those roles can be lived out on the local, national and international stage. There are levels of increasing depth for new, growing and mature Christians.

All sorts of people from all walks of life become involved in church *Foundations21* groups, as it meets a need in churches, offering innovative and thoughtful methods for nurturing anyone—from people taking first steps in faith to leaders looking to revitalize and replenish their faith.

Foundations21 uses the booming world of technology to bring together those who might otherwise remain on the fringes of church life. Those who might be unable to participate in church activities because of unsociable working hours have found that they can log on at the time that suits them. People who can't get out and about to church events can meet and chat online or on the phone.

The emphasis *Foundations21* places on both online and personal contact enables people from all walks of life to be included, and it is simple enough for even those technophobes among us to use with ease.

With all this going on, *Foundations21* has a great deal to offer churches. Not only does it offer a platform for spiritual growth but, with readymade group material such as DVD clips, discussion starters and the beginnings of a sermon series (how about spending one month on each of the twelve topics?), it also weaves discipleship into the core fabric of the church.

A number of churches have now opted to take part, running *Foundations21* groups as part of their regular activities. One church leader who has taken up this opportunity remarked:

26 years ago, I became a Christian and was given a foundation of discipleship that has made me eternally grateful. My prayer is that the experience people are being brought into today with Foundations21 will result in the same feeling of thanks and appreciation in many years to come.

Let's make it our aim that ongoing discipleship will be going on in every part of our lives, as the writer of Hebrews exhorts us, 'Let us… spur one another on towards love and good deeds. Let us not give up meeting together' (10:24–25).

To subscribe to Foundations21, *please turn to the form on page 157.*

Sharon Durant joined the BRF team in 2005 as a member of the marketing team and was part of the BRF Foundations21 *pilot group in 2006.*

BRF in Abingdon

Lisa Cherrett

At the end of August 2007, Bible Reading Fellowship completed the purchase of new offices in Abingdon, five miles south of Oxford. The new HQ is close to the town centre and provides BRF and its team of 24 staff with much-needed additional space and scope for further growth in the future.

Packing began some weeks before the move, after a thorough clear-out of the old equipment and stationery that accumulates even in the best-organized offices and homes. On 29 and 30 August, 15 The Chambers started to fill up with carefully labelled boxes and furniture. By the next day, desks and shelves had been installed, books and files had found their new places, and computers had been connected.

The office is on three levels. The second floor houses the editorial department, with marketing and customer services below on the first floor. The ground floor provides ample space for a large meeting room, post and stock room, and kitchen.

As a member of the editorial team, working on the top floor, the biggest difference I've noticed between the new offices and the old is the quietness of the new surroundings. The offices BRF leased

for seven years in Oxford were next to the A40, the city's ringroad, bombarded with constant traffic noise and the sound of sirens from emergency vehicles travelling to and from the local hospitals. In Abingdon, set apart from the main roads and overlooking a small courtyard car park, the most noticeable outdoor sound is the occasional cooing of a pigeon—much more conducive to concentration.

Bishop Colin Fletcher, BRF's Chairman of Trustees, has commented, 'As trustees we have been delighted to see the many ways in which God has blessed BRF's ministry over the years. This move represents the opening of another new chapter for the organization and we are excited about what lies ahead.' Those of us who work here echo those thoughts as we have quickly settled into BRF's permanent new home.

15 THE CHAMBERS, ABINGDON

EDITORIAL DEPARTMENT, TOP FLOOR

Lisa Cherrett is BRF's Project Editor and Managing Editor for the Bible reading notes.

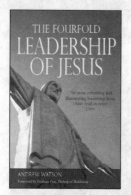

An extract from *The Fourfold Leadership of Jesus*

'Don't follow me. Follow Jesus!' runs a popular slogan, while Paul wrote, 'Follow my example, as I follow the example of Christ.' As leaders, can we ever hope to echo Paul's words—or should we only point away from ourselves to Jesus? In this book, Andrew Watson explores what it means to lead as Jesus led, as he called his disciples to come, to follow, to wait and to go. Those four commands embody the four different aspects of leadership that this book explores as a model for us today. The following extract is an abridged version of Chapter 1, 'Accessible leadership'.

One of the historical oddities referred to in E.H. Gombrich's magnificent book *The Story of Art* is the number of aesthetic movements that were first 'christened' by the critics who derided them. The word 'Gothic', for example, was initially used by Italian art critics to denote a style that they considered barbarous, brought into Italy by the Goths who had effectively destroyed the Roman empire and true culture with it… 'Mannerism' and 'Impressionism' were also terms coined by their opponents, and although the first exhibition held by the Impressionists was widely ridiculed… it wasn't long before Monet and his friends were wearing the Impressionist badge with pride.

The same may be said of the expression 'Friend of tax collectors and sinners'—a term of abuse used by Jesus' opponents but one that Jesus himself never tried to repudiate. Jesus' only response to the accusation in Matthew 11:19 is that 'wisdom is proved right by her actions'. His reputation as a man who actively sought out the more disreputable members of the society around him provided constant fuel for a growing swell of gossip and censure instigated by the religious leaders of his day…

The sheer accessibility of Jesus' leadership is evident from the moment we first pick up a Gospel. 'Come to me,' said Jesus, and they came—synagogue rulers, royal officials, Pharisees and members of the Jewish ruling council; tax collectors, lepers, unspecified 'sinners' and women with unmentionable diseases; parents wanting Jesus to bless their little children and mothers seeking preferment for their big children, as well as... Roman centurions, Samaritans, Canaanites, Greeks and some exotic visitors from the east, bearing gifts of gold, frankincense and myrrh...

Why, then, was he willing to associate with quite such mixed and frequently unsavoury company? Why was he ready to court such hostility for the stand he took on this particular issue? The answer is that accessibility lay at the very heart of the mission to which Jesus knew himself to be called. He was the Son of Man, come to seek and to save the lost. He was the shepherd called to find the sheep that had strayed. He was the doctor whose availability to the sick was integral to his sense of vocation (Luke 19:10; 15:4; Matthew 9:12). In response to his opponents, Jesus would sometimes use the word 'sinner' as they did, but his own preference was to speak the non-pejorative language of lostness and disease. For the shepherd to ignore the sheep who had strayed, or for the doctor to keep his distance from the patients who so desperately needed him, would have been the gravest dereliction of duty, the most basic disregard of the call to pastor and to heal.

There are many reasons, of course, why leaders frequently like to keep their distance. Shyness, privacy, stress, busyness: all play their part in building an invisible barrier between the leader and those who are led, while the question of leadership priorities becomes particularly acute as an organization begins to grow. But practicalities like these were not responsible for the outrage with which Jesus' radical accessibility was greeted. Underlying that anger lay two basic values to which his opponents were variously committed: the cultivation of leadership mystique on the one hand, and the commitment to ritual purity on the other.

Misleadership: mystique and ritual purity

'Mystique' was a concept that the classical world inherited from Persia... As John Adair puts it, it was the Persians who had 'introduced prostration as part of a novel method of creating an aura of divinity around their kings'. This 'aura of divinity' was maintained through the remoteness of the king from his people, and found expression in the increasingly elaborate palaces, courtyards and protective walls that bedecked the ancient world...

Classical culture had a contrary tradition, too, in which a leader made himself accessible to his people... The Greek historian Flavius Arrianus describes how the young Alexander the Great showed deep concern for the wounded after one of the battles in his Persian campaign: 'He visited them all,' writes Arrianus, 'and examined their wounds, asking each man how and in what circumstances his wound was received, and allowing him to tell the story and exaggerate as much as he pleased'! But even Alexander, that exemplary model of motivational leadership, seems to have been progressively seduced by the Persian approach. John Adair charts his growing self-importance in later years, fuelled by flattering courtiers, both Greek and Persian, who puffed up his pretensions to be a living god…

Caesar Augustus, introduced to us at the beginning of Luke's Gospel, had largely bought into the culture of 'mystique': the name 'Augustus' ('exalted') is a simple reminder of that fact. Even the puppet-king Herod Agrippa happily received the adulation of his people ('This is the voice of a god, not of a mere mortal', Acts 12:22) and died five days later in an incident that both Luke and the Jewish historian Josephus regarded as an act of divine retribution. Against this background it is hardly surprising that the accessibility of Jesus did not endear him to his Roman hearers. Jesus' words in Mark 10:42, 'Those who are regarded as rulers of the Gentiles lord it over them, and their high officials exercise

authority over them', prove that he would never see eye-to-eye with his Roman contemporaries on leadership issues…

While mystique was part of the Roman world of Jesus' day, the Jewish culture was far more focused on the theme of ritual purity. Taking their lead from the holiness code in the Torah… and amplifying the Torah's regulations with a hundred-and-one fiddly bylaws, the Pharisees were outraged at the laxity of Jesus and the dangers of moral contagion from the company he kept. Simon the Pharisee's response to the embarrassing gatecrasher who wiped the feet of Jesus with ointment and tears is typical of this approach: 'If this man were a prophet, he would know who is touching him and what kind of woman she is—that she is a sinner' (Luke 7:39). The beginning of that sentence—'If this man were a prophet'—suggests that even the more sympathetic of the Pharisees regarded Jesus' radical accessibility as a major stumbling block to their acceptance of his authority as one sent by God.

Jesus' response to such criticism has already been noted, and the 'doctor' image is especially suggestive. Yes, evil can be contagious: it can infect us like yeast 'infects' a batch of dough (see

> *Caesar Augustus had largely bought into the culture of 'mystique'*

Jesus' warning in Matthew 16:6). But goodness—the power of the kingdom to forgive, restore, transform and heal—is more contagious still. Jesus never underestimated the grip of sin in our lives as some more liberal commentators are prone to do: 'everyone who sins is a slave to sin', as he put it bluntly in John 8:34. Yet the Spirit's anointing to 'proclaim freedom for the prisoners and recovery of sight for the blind' (Luke 4:18) most clearly rested upon him, and with it came a completely new approach to holiness, which was proactive, not reactive; faithful, not fearful; on the front foot, not constantly in retreat. The great commission of Matthew 28 would perhaps have been fulfilled by now had only the Church emulated our Lord's example.

With it came a completely new approach to holiness

Jesus the shepherd

In contrast to these misleaders, Jesus' call to 'come to me' took its cue from a deep biblical image: the picture of God as shepherd alongside the 'under-shepherding' of prophet, priest and king. The good shepherd in this image was one who gathered the sheep to himself. The bad shepherd was consistently responsible for their scattering.

Having bad shepherds was tantamount to having no shepherds at all, as the prophet Micaiah was bold enough to remind weak King Ahab. 'I saw all Israel scattered on the hills like sheep without a shepherd', he announced, earning for himself Ahab's grumpy response, 'Didn't I tell you that he never prophesies anything good about me, but only bad?' The context of this story is also instructive, with Ahab having gathered the people to fight the king of Aram. In the absence of a good shepherd-king (one modelled on the life of David), Micaiah warned Ahab that such attempts to gather were inappropriate. Instead Ahab should let the Israelites disperse, scatter…

Moving from (arguably) the worst shepherd in the Old Testament to (unarguably) the best, the most tender example of 'Come to me' leadership appears in a famous passage in Isaiah 40. There it is said of God himself, 'He tends his flock like a shepherd: he gathers the lambs in his arms and carries them close to his heart; he gently leads those that have young' (v. 11)…

In the New Testament, this gathering imagery, in a startlingly feminine form, is a feature of Jesus' leadership in his lament over Jerusalem: 'Jerusalem, Jerusalem… how often I have longed to gather your children together, as a hen gathers her chicks under her wings, but you were not willing' (Matthew 23:37). His image of the good shepherd who 'calls his own sheep by name' (John 10:3) is similarly powerful... And Jesus didn't simply speak in such terms. Time and time again, he practised what he preached, gathering the most unlikely group of people to himself, frequently around a meal table.

The most famous 'Come to me' invitation of them all is also the most illuminating. 'Come to me,' said Jesus, 'all you who are weary and burdened, and I will give you rest. Take my yoke upon you and learn from me, for I am gentle and humble in heart, and you will find rest for your souls. For my yoke is easy and my burden is light' (Matthew 11:28–30).

Of course, many people are weary and burdened, and a hundred Christian generations have rightly found comfort in this warm and winsome invitation. But Jesus may have had a particular type of hearer in mind when he issued it—not simply those who were wearied by life in general but those who were burdened by the incessant demands of the religious leaders, with their intrusive interpretations of the law. As he said later of the Pharisees, 'They tie up heavy, cumbersome loads and put them on other people's shoulders, but they themselves are not willing to lift a finger to move them' (Matthew 23:4).

The 'yoke' of the law was later mentioned in the critical discussions of the Council of Jerusalem. In debating the question of the Church's accessibility to its growing Gentile membership, Peter wisely posed the question, 'Why do you try to test God by putting on the necks of Gentiles a yoke that neither we nor our ancestors have been able to bear?' (Acts 15:10). It's hardly surprising, then, that Jesus' gracious invitation to lay down that burden and replace it with an 'easy' yoke (perhaps in the sense of being fit for use and tailor-made for the wearer) was to prove so attractive.

It might seem ill-advised to seek to rehabilitate a much-derided children's hymn at this point. But the verse, 'Gentle Jesus, meek and mild, look upon a little child' picks up some of the major traits of 'Come to me' leadership rather well, whatever its sentimental associations. Gentleness, meekness, mildness—or, to modernize the words a little, gentleness, humility and a peaceable spirit—join compassion and vulnerability as key qualities in the character of Jesus, and these virtues help to explain the radical accessibility which was to prove such a significant feature of his ministry. It is to these 'come to me' qualities that we now turn.

To order a copy of this book, please turn to the order form on page 159.

The Editor recommends

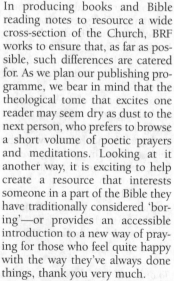

Naomi Starkey

As we seek to grow in faith, to travel further along the discipleship road, it is important to remember that what encourages and builds up one person may actually have little impact on another, or may even discourage them. Our personalities—the fact that God created us as unique individuals—means that our ways of learning, worshipping and sharing our faith are often very different from those of family, friends and fellow church members.

In producing books and Bible reading notes to resource a wide cross-section of the Church, BRF works to ensure that, as far as possible, such differences are catered for. As we plan our publishing programme, we bear in mind that the theological tome that excites one reader may seem dry as dust to the next person, who prefers to browse a short volume of poetic prayers and meditations. Looking at it another way, it is exciting to help create a resource that interests someone in a part of the Bible they have traditionally considered 'boring'—or provides an accessible introduction to a new way of praying for those who feel quite happy with the way they've always done things, thank you very much.

For many people, hearing about 'how it happened to me' is a powerful way of learning more of how and why God works. *Six Men—Encountering God* is a book of stories shared by six individuals, each of whom, in different ways and at different times, came 'face to face with God'. As a result, their lives were never the same again.

Reading the book, we meet the rock climber facing a certain-to-be-fatal fall, the wheeler-dealer whose fortunes crash disastrously, and the cynic whose prejudices are confounded when the Holy Spirit gets to work. Along with the other men featured, they share a pivotal experience, either a moment of crisis or a process of gradual realization, when they recognize a 'God-shaped gap' within.

Six Men—Encountering God is both a call to continue to seek God ourselves (and give thanks for the relationship with him that we already have) and an inspiration and encouragement to marriage partners, family or church members who are longing for a particular person to come to faith. As each story unfolds, the part played by prayer and faithful, low-key witness is shown time and again to be crucial in nudging somebody towards the kingdom, even if the timescale involved is a long one.

Author Brad Lincoln is now a company director but previously spent five years working in Nepal with his family, where he oversaw the International Nepal Fellowship's work in the western region of the country. He has written his book for those who feel they know God well and want to get better acquainted with how he works in people's lives—but also for those who may doubt that God exists at all. Both the book and its author are warmly endorsed in a foreword by former South African rugby captain François Pienaar, who shares something of his own path to Christian faith.

While this story-based book provides a dramatic way of reflecting on whether or not faith works, *Seeking Faith, Finding God* by John Rackley offers a more measured approach. Subtitled 'Getting to grips with questions of faith', John's book grew out of the popular 'Rackley's Reflections' column that he has contributed to *The Baptist Times* over recent years.

Grouped in five sections (A yearning faith; A gospel place; Gospel encounters; Faith companions; Praying the gospel), the pithy Bible-based reflections are based around a fundamental question: what does it mean to be a disciple of Jesus, living according to his gospel in today's world? John is keen to show the importance of developing a 'seeking and searching' faith if we want to be effective witnesses to what we believe.

The society around us continues to change rapidly, sometimes for the better, often for the worse; we live in 'difficult and demanding times', as John points out. The challenge before us is to find ways of explaining what we know to be true to a world that is not only confident that the Church has little to offer but also profoundly ignorant of God's revelation.

Seeking Faith, Finding God is a book that lends itself to group reading and discussion, and is also commended by Paddy Lane of the Retreat Association. As we read it, we are reminded of the importance of holding on to questions and being honest in our struggle to understand and believe what the Bible tells us. In so doing, we are better able to connect with those outside or on the fringes of the Church. They may yearn to come further in but fear that their faith is insufficient; they need to hear Jesus' gentle words about the size of a mustard seed.

To order either of these books, please turn to the order form on page 159.

An extract from
Footsteps to the Feast

In *Footsteps to the Feast*, Martyn Payne offers the opportunity to explore the 'big story' of God's purpose for his world through twelve fun-filled two-hour special events. Each programme is packed with tried and tested ideas including icebreakers, games, drama, music and crafts, and at the heart of each event there is space for visual storytelling and reflection. The programmes explore the feasts and festivals of Advent, Holy Week, Harvest, Epiphany, Pentecost, Hallowe'en and All Saints, Candlemas, Trinity, St Michael and All Angels, Lent, The early Church and Bible Sunday. The following is an extract from '3–2–1 Go! A special event for the feast of Trinity'.

The feast of Trinity comes on the Sunday immediately after Pentecost and celebrates the mystery of God as three persons in one. Christians describe the fullness of God using the formula 'God the Father, God the Son and God the Holy Spirit'. This understanding of God is drawn from the teachings of the Bible and the life and words of Jesus in particular.

It is not an easy concept for adults, let alone children, to understand, and for many outside the Christian faith it can seem as if Christians are worshipping not one God but three. This is a particular stumbling block to Jews and Muslims, who firmly believe that there is only one God. In fact, Christians believe this too, but they see God in action in three distinct ways: as the creator, the redeemer and the sanctifier. They believe that the hidden face of God the Father was made visible on earth as Jesus, and that the life of God the Son is experienced in Christians as the Holy Spirit, who is the invisible God living inside people.

The Trinity is the Church's attempt to embrace the experience of these three elements of the Godhead, and celebrates this fuller understanding of the true character of God. The feast of Trinity reminds each of us that we owe our existence, our salvation and the possibility of new life and change to this reality. What follows is a two-hour programme to present this truth in some lively and memorable ways using story, games, craft and drama.

Here is a way of telling the story of the baptism of Jesus with all the children together, inviting them to get involved in some simple drama. For props, you will need a blue sheet, something camel-coloured for John to wear and a simple drape for Jesus. Gather the children in a circle, but with a good clear space in the middle where the action will take place.

Introduce the story by laying across the circle the blue sheet folded into a long, thin strip. Begin the story with the words 'Something strange was happening down by the river. Someone was shouting at the top of his voice.'

Invite someone to play the part of John. This person needs to have a good shouting voice! Teach them this line: 'Change your ways! Get ready for the Lord!'

Practise this several times loudly and, as each new piece of the drama is added, return to the character of John to hear this message shouted again.

Continue with the story by saying, 'All sorts of people heard that something strange was going on down by the river and so they all came to see for themselves.'

You will now need five groups of people (of whatever numbers you can manage, according to the total size of your group). Introduce each of these groups, one at a time, and make sure they each establish their actions and words before the next group is introduced. Don't forget, in between each group, to return to John to hear him shouting his message for everyone. If possible, assign an adult leader to each group to prompt their words and movements.

❂ **Group 1: the soldiers:** This group should march around the circle using the chant 'Left, right; left, right; do what we tell you.'

❂ **Group 2: the tax collectors:** This group should creep around the circle using the chant 'Money from him, money from her; all the more for me.'

❂ **Group 3: ordinary people:** This group should walk around the circle shaking their heads selfishly with the chant 'This is mine and not for you; I'll keep it for myself.'

❂ **Group 4: the Pharisees:** This group should walk tall and proudly around the circle to the chant of 'We're God's chosen; so listen to us.'

❂ **Group 5: the king and his court:** This group should stay in one place and keep their distance from John with the chant 'I'll do what I like, so go take a hike!'

As the story unfolds, introduce the arrival of each group punctuated by the shouting from John. Build this up so that it becomes a real chorus of chants and shouting. Something very strange was going on by the river!

Say, 'John demanded that each group should change their ways.' Ask the children how they think each of the groups could change their ways. What might John have said to them? Perhaps it might have been something like 'Don't bully others', 'Don't be greedy', 'Don't be selfish' and so on. Ask the children to suggest what other things John might have said.

Some of the people did change their ways. To show this, take one or two from each of the groups up to John in turn. They should bow down and be covered by the blue sheet for a short moment—being 'baptized' as a sign that they want to change and be different. John could say the words 'Be baptized and get ready for the Lord.' Some from each of the groups should be 'baptized', but the group around the king do not get involved. You might mention that the king (King Herod) was so angry with what John was saying about him that eventually he arrested John and put him into prison.

While these baptisms were going on, something else very strange happened. John's cousin Jesus appeared (choose someone to play the part of Jesus). Jesus went right up to John, who was standing in the water, and asked John to baptize him. John was shocked because he recognized that Jesus was the 'Lord' he was talking about. John told Jesus that he, John, should be the one to be baptized by Jesus. But Jesus said that, for now, it should be the other way around.

Invite the child chosen to play the part of Jesus to bend down and be covered by the blue sheet of water as he is 'baptized'. Describe to the children what was heard and seen when this happened. There was a voice from heaven ('This is my own dear Son and I am pleased with him') and the Spirit of God in the form of a dove alighted upon Jesus. You could emphasize this with some appropriate actions for the dove and by cupping your hands around your mouth to make a 'microphone' for God's words. The three sides to the character of God were together in one place: Father, Son and Holy Spirit.

Jesus was very special. The people nearby saw his baptism and began to follow Jesus rather than John. John had done his work. At the conclusion of the story, ask the following questions:

- ❂ I wonder how John felt as he baptized his cousin, Jesus?
- ❂ I wonder what the crowds made of the voice and the dove?
- ❂ I wonder what John was thinking as he saw people start to follow Jesus and not him?
- ❂ I wonder if the crowds understood that God was in the voice, in the dove and in Jesus?

To order a copy of this book, please turn to the order form on page 159.

New Daylight © BRF 2008

The Bible Reading Fellowship
15 The Chambers, Vineyard, Abingdon OX14 3FE
Tel: 01865 319700; Fax: 01865 319701
E-mail: enquiries@brf.org.uk; Website: www.brf.org.uk

ISBN 978 1 84101 474 6

Distributed in Australia by:
Willow Connection, PO Box 288, Brookvale, NSW 2100.
Tel: 02 9948 3957; Fax: 02 9948 8153;
E-mail: info@willowconnection.com.au
Available also from all good Christian bookshops in Australia.
For individual and group subscriptions in Australia:
Mrs Rosemary Morrall, PO Box W35, Wanniassa, ACT 2903.

Distributed in New Zealand by:
Scripture Union Wholesale, PO Box 760, Wellington
Tel: 04 385 0421; Fax: 04 384 3990; E-mail: suwholesale@clear.net.nz

Distributed in Canada by:
The Anglican Book Centre, 80 Hayden Street, Toronto, Ontario, M4Y 3G2
Tel: 001 416 924-1332; Fax: 001 416 924-2760;
E-mail: abc@anglicanbookcentre.com; Website: www.anglicanbookcentre.com

Publications distributed to more than 60 countries

Acknowledgments
The New Revised Standard Version of the Bible, Anglicized Edition, copyright © 1989, 1995 by the
Division of Christian Education of the National Council of the Churches of Christ in the USA. Used
by permission. All rights reserved.

The Holy Bible, New International Version, copyright © 1973, 1978, 1984 by International Bible
Society. Used by permission of Hodder & Stoughton Publishers, a division of Hodder Headline Ltd.
All rights reserved. 'NIV' is a registered trademark of International Bible Society. UK trademark
number 1448790.

The Holy Bible, Today's New International Version, copyright © 2004 by International Bible Society.
Used by permission of Hodder & Stoughton Publishers, a division of Hodder Headline Ltd. All
rights reserved. 'TNIV' is a registered trademark of International Bible Society.

Extracts from the Authorized Version of the Bible (The King James Bible), the rights in which are
vested in the Crown, are reproduced by permission of the Crown's Patentee, Cambridge University
Press.

The Revised Common Lectionary is copyright © The Consultation on Common Texts, 1992 and is
reproduced with permission. *The Christian Year: Calendar, Lectionary and Collects*, which includes the
Common Worship lectionary (the Church of England's adaptations of the *Revised Common Lectionary*,
published as the Principal Service lectionary) is copyright © The Central Board of Finance of the
Church of England, 1995, 1997, and material from it is reproduced with permission.

Printed in Singapore by Craft Print International Ltd

BRF is a Christian charity committed to resourcing the spiritual journey of adults and children alike. For adults, BRF publishes Bible reading notes and books and offers an annual programme of quiet days and retreats. Under its children's imprint *Barnabas*, BRF publishes a wide range of books for those working with children under 11 in school, church and home. BRF's *Barnabas Ministry* team offers INSET sessions for primary teachers, training for children's leaders in church, quiet days, and a range of events to enable children themselves to engage with the Bible and its message.

We need your help if we are to make a real impact on the local church and community. In an increasingly secular world people need even more help with their Bible reading, their prayer and their discipleship. We can do something about this, but our resources are limited. With your help, if we all do a little, together we can make a huge difference.

How can you help?

• You could support BRF's ministry with a donation or standing order (using the response form overleaf).

• You could consider making a bequest to BRF in your will, and so give lasting support to our work. (We have a leaflet available with more information about this, which can be requested using the form overleaf.)

• And, most important of all, you could support BRF with your prayers.

Whatever you can do or give, we thank you for your support.

BRF – resourcing your spiritual journey

BRF MINISTRY APPEAL RESPONSE FORM

Name _____

Address _____

_____ Postcode _____

Telephone _____ Email _____

(tick as appropriate)

Gift Aid Declaration

☐ I am a UK taxpayer. I want BRF to treat as Gift Aid Donations all donations I
make from 6 April 2000 until I notify you otherwise.

Signature _____ Date _____

☐ I would like to support BRF's ministry with a regular donation by standing order
(please complete the Banker's Order below).

Standing Order – Banker's Order

To the Manager, Name of Bank/Building Society _____

Address _____

_____ Postcode _____

Sort Code _____ Account Name _____

Account No _____

Please pay Royal Bank of Scotland plc, Drummonds, 49 Charing Cross,
London SW1A 2DX (Sort Code 16-00-38), for the account of BRF A/C No. 00774151

The sum of _____ pounds on ___ /___ /___ (insert date your standing order starts)
and thereafter the same amount on the same day of each month until further notice.

Signature _____ Date _____

Single donation

☐ I enclose my cheque/credit card/Switch card details for a donation of
£5 £10 £25 £50 £100 £250 (other) £ _____ to support BRF's ministry

Credit/Switch card no. ☐☐☐☐ ☐☐☐☐ ☐☐☐☐ ☐☐☐☐ ☐☐☐☐ ☐☐☐☐

Expires ☐☐☐☐ Security code ☐☐☐ Issue no. of Switch card ☐☐☐☐

Signature _____ Date _____

(Where appropriate, on receipt of your donation, we will send you a Gift Aid form)

☐ Please send me information about making a bequest to BRF in my will.

Please detach and send this completed form to: Richard Fisher, BRF,
15 The Chambers, Vineyard, Abingdon OX14 3FE. BRF is a Registered Charity (No.233280)

ND0208

FOUNDATIONS21 SUBSCRIPTION

Name _____

Address _____

_____ Postcode _____

Telephone _____ Email _____

	Quantity	Price	Total
Foundations21 45-day trial membership pack Includes a DVD of video clips for Room 1 (Jesus), Disciple Master DVD Room 1 (Jesus), unlimited online membership for 45 days.	_____	£7.99	_____
Foundations21 annual subscription Includes a DVD of video clips for Rooms 1-12, Disciple Master DVD Rooms 1-12 and unlimited online membership for a year.	_____	£59.00	_____

To be able to use Foundations21 you will need the following minimum system requirements on your computer: Pentium III - 500 Mhz processor, 64MB RAM (128 or higher recommended), Audio capability, Windows 98SE/XP, Internet Explorer 6, DVD-ROM drive, Internet connection (preferably broadband).

You will also need: Java™ Virtual Machine for Windows®, Microsoft® Windows® Media Player, Macromedia® Flash® Player for Windows®. These are already installed on many computers or can be downloaded FREE from the Internet.

Total enclosed £ _____(cheques should be made payable to 'BRF')

Payment by cheque ❏ postal order ❏ Visa ❏ Mastercard ❏ Switch ❏

Credit/Switch card no. ❏❏❏❏❏❏❏❏❏❏❏❏❏❏❏❏❏❏❏❏

Expires ❏❏❏❏ Security code ❏❏❏ Issue no. of Switch card ❏❏❏❏

Signature (essential if paying by credit/Switch card)_____

Foundations21 **is available by monthly payments and at special rates for groups. Visit www.foundations21.org.uk**

BRF, 15 The Chambers, Vineyard, Abingdon OX14 3FE. BRF is a Registered Charity

❏ Please send me a Bible reading resources pack to encourage Bible reading in my church

❏ I would like to take out a subscription myself (complete your name and address details only once)

❏ I would like to give a gift subscription (please complete both name and address sections below)

Your name _____

Your address _____

_____ Postcode _____

Gift subscription name _____

Gift subscription address _____

_____ Postcode _____

Please send *New Daylight* beginning with the September 2008 / January / May 2009 issue: (delete as applicable)

(please tick box)	UK	SURFACE	AIR MAIL
NEW DAYLIGHT	❏ £13.35	❏ £14.55	❏ £16.65
NEW DAYLIGHT 3-year sub	❏ £30.00		
NEW DAYLIGHT DELUXE	❏ £17.25	❏ £21.60	❏ £26.70

I would like to take out an annual subscription to *Quiet Spaces* beginning with the next available issue:

(please tick box)	UK	SURFACE	AIR MAIL
QUIET SPACES	❏ £16.95	❏ £18.45	❏ £20.85

Please complete the payment details below and send your coupon, with appropriate payment, to:
BRF, 15 The Chambers, Vineyard, Abingdon OX14 3FE.

Total enclosed £ _____ (cheques should be made payable to 'BRF')

Payment by cheque ❏ postal order ❏ Visa ❏ Mastercard ❏ Switch ❏

Card number: ☐☐☐☐ ☐☐☐☐ ☐☐☐☐ ☐☐☐☐

Expires: ☐☐☐☐ Security code ☐☐☐ Issue no (Switch): ☐☐☐☐

Signature (essential if paying by credit/Switch card) _____

BRF is a Registered Charity

BRF PUBLICATIONS ORDER FORM

Please ensure that you complete and send off both sides of this order form.

Please send me the following book(s):

		Quantity	Price	Total
581 1	The Path of Celtic Prayer (C. Miller)	_____	£6.99	_____
545 3	The Starship Discovery Holiday Club (J. Hardwick)	_____	£8.99	_____
435 7	The Fourfold Leadership of Jesus (A. Watson)	_____	£7.99	_____
528 6	Six Men—Encountering God (B. Lincoln)	_____	£7.99	_____
543 9	Seeking Faith—Finding God (J. Rackley)	_____	£6.99	_____
464 7	Footsteps to the Feast (M. Payne)	_____	£8.99	_____
314 5	PBC: Genesis (G. West)	_____	£8.99	_____
095 3	PBC: Joshua & Judges (S.D. Mathewson)	_____	£7.99	_____
242 1	PBC: Ruth, Esther, Ecclesiastes, Song, Lamentations (R. Fyall)	_____	£8.99	_____
118 9	PBC: 1 & 2 Kings (S.B. Dawes)	_____	£7.99	_____
040 3	PBC: Ezekiel (E. Lucas)	_____	£7.99	_____
191 2	PBC: Matthew (J. Proctor)	_____	£8.99	_____
029 8	PBC: John (R.A. Burridge)	_____	£8.99	_____
216 2	PBC: Acts (L. Alexander)	_____	£8.99	_____
536 9	PBC: 1 Corinthians (J. Murphy-O'Connor)	_____	£7.99	_____
119 6	PBC: Timothy, Titus and Hebrews (D. France)	_____	£7.99	_____

POSTAGE AND PACKING CHARGES				
order value	UK	Europe	Surface	Air Mail
£7.00 & under	£1.25	£3.00	£3.50	£5.50
£7.01–£30.00	£2.25	£5.50	£6.50	£10.00
Over £30.00	free	prices on request		

Total cost of books £ _____
Donation £ _____
Postage and packing £ _____
TOTAL £ _____

See over for payment details. All prices are correct at time of going to press, are subject to the prevailing rate of VAT and may be subject to change without prior warning.

PAYMENT DETAILS

Please complete the payment details below and send with appropriate payment and completed order form to:

**BRF, 15 The Chambers, Vineyard,
Abingdon OX14 3FE**

Name _____

Address _____

_____

_____ Postcode _____

Telephone _____

Email _____

Total enclosed £ _____ (cheques should be made payable to 'BRF')

Payment by cheque ❏ postal order ❏ Visa ❏ Mastercard ❏ Switch ❏

Card number: ⬚⬚⬚⬚⬚⬚⬚⬚⬚⬚⬚⬚⬚⬚⬚⬚⬚⬚⬚⬚⬚⬚

Expires: ⬚⬚⬚⬚ Security code ⬚⬚⬚ Issue no (Switch): ⬚⬚⬚⬚

Signature (essential if paying by credit/Switch card) _____

❏ Please do not send me further information about BRF publications.

ALTERNATIVE WAYS TO ORDER

Christian bookshops: All good Christian bookshops stock BRF publications. For your nearest stockist, please contact BRF.

Telephone: The BRF office is open between 09.15 and 17.30.
To place your order, phone 01865 319700; fax 01865 319701.

Web: Visit www.brf.org.uk

ND0208